"*Lost Women of Turkey* is part history lesson, part pilgrimage, and wholly an invitation. With honesty about her own questions of marriage, work, identity, and faith, Beth shows us how the ancient stories of women intersect with our modern lives, how hidden influence and quiet authority have always been part of women's power, and how God still speaks through the strangeness of foreign soil. Beth is a masterful guide and an experienced pilgrim. This book will not only change the way you see history—it will change the way you see yourself."

—BEKAH STEWART, AUTHOR *PERMISSION TO MATTER: RECLAIMING WOMEN'S HUMANITY & AUTHORITY AT THE INVITATION OF JESUS*

"Through an artistic integration of biblical narrative, church history, and personal story, Beth invites us to listen to the lost voices of women in Turkey in order to uncover deep connections among us all. Our own voices are uncovered and empowered as we pilgrimage with her, gazing at the art of ancient churches in Turkey, feeling the heat and cold of the Turkish bath on our bodies, and creating eternal community through shared stories and recipes. You will laugh, cry, and be transformed as you read *The Lost Women of Turkey*!"

—REV. AMY F DAVIS ABDALLAH, PH.D., PROFESSOR, PILGRIMAGE LEADER, AUTHOR OF *MEANING IN THE MOMENT* AND *THE BOOK OF WOMANHOOD*

"In *Lost Women of Turkey*, Beth Bruno leads readers through a sacred landscape into kitchens fragrant with ancient recipes, ruins humming with prayers of forgotten saints, and her own soul in search of a deepening spirituality. Weaving memoir, history, and spiritual imagination, she blends travel with transformation. Through Bruno's compelling prose readers meet and draw inspiration from women who shaped Christian memory—saints, mothers, martyrs—in a work that goes beyond words on a page to a full-on sensory experience. Highly recommend!"

—SANDRA GLAHN, SEMINARY PROFESSOR, AUTHOR
OF *NOBODY'S MOTHER: ARTEMIS OF THE EPHESIANS
IN ANTIQUITY AND THE NEW TESTAMENT*

"Beth is part storyteller, part sleuth, part priestess—wholly brilliant. With a heart tuned to mystery and a scholar's eye for detail, she becomes your trusted guide through the bustling streets and historical sites of Istanbul, the surreal topography of Cappadocia, and the windswept ruins of Ephesus. In *Lost Women of Turkey*, Beth walks beside you, inviting you to taste the spice of their culture, to feel history hum beneath your feet, and to uncover the long-buried fragments of your own feminine soul that have been waiting, quietly, for this moment of return. This book is your invitation to travel with her into the depths of Turkey, but more importantly into the deep places of your sacred story."

—TRACY JOHNSON, STORYWORK SUPERVISOR AT RESTORY
COUNSELING AND CO-LEADER OF *LOST WOMEN PILGRIMAGES*

"Beth Bruno's breathtaking descriptions lure us into a world unfamiliar to most of us, but one that has become a spiritual home for her. And because she has spent so much of her life residing and leading in Turkey, we can trust her guidance. In this book she invites us to be virtual pilgrims with her, to walk roads that the earliest Christians would have walked; to breathe in spicy, aromatic scents; to be open to the possibility of friendships, though our languages and cultures could not be more different. And to dare to ask questions of ourselves that will stretch and nurture our sanctified imaginations. This is a book that asks for our participation, and as readers, we are greatly rewarded."

—TRACY BALZER, AUTHOR OF *A JOURNEY OF SEA AND STONE: HOW HOLY PLACES GUIDE AND RENEW US*

"Beth Bruno invites us into a magical land and an unforgettable journey—a pilgrimage through time and space. Her writing opens a fresh imagination of God and of the women who have gone before us, calling us to remember, to learn, and to practice a life worth living. This book is a gift and a joy to read."

—CATHY LOERZEL, CO-AUTHOR OF *REDEEMING HEARTACHE* AND CO-FOUNDER OF THE ALLENDER CENTER

LOST WOMEN of TURKEY

On *On* MAKING PILGRIMAGE *and* FINDING SELF

BETH BRUNO

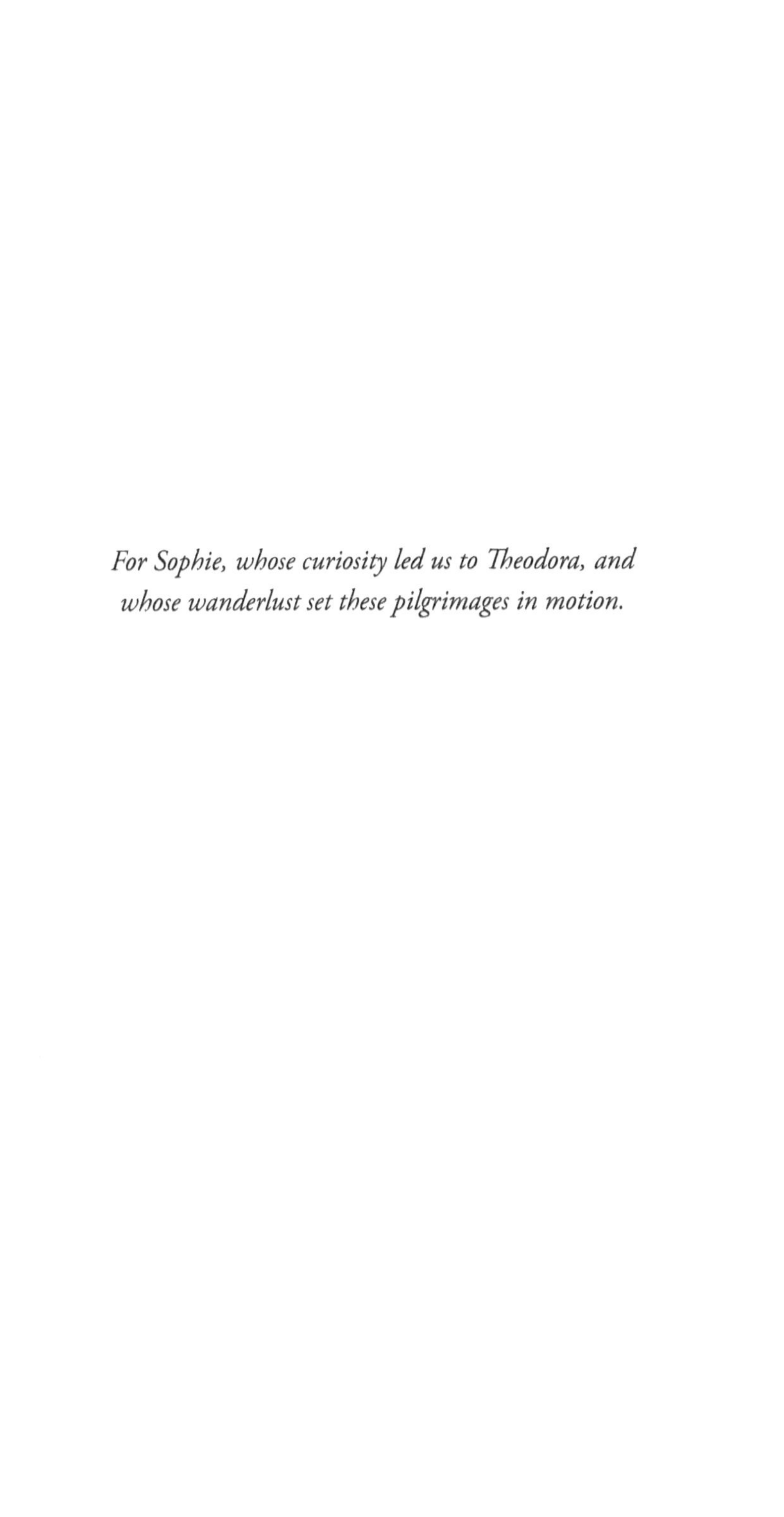

For Sophie, whose curiosity led us to Theodora, and whose wanderlust set these pilgrimages in motion.

"A pilgrimage is a ritual journey with a hallowed purpose. Every step along the way has meaning. The pilgrim knows that the journey will be difficult and that life-giving challenges will emerge. A pilgrimage is not a vacation; it is a transformational journey during which significant change takes place. New insights are given. Deeper understanding is attained. New and old places in the heart are visited. Blessings are received. Healing takes place. On return from pilgrimage, life is seen with different eyes. Nothing will ever be quite the same again."

— MACRINA WIEDERKEHR

BEHOLD YOUR LIFE

"Dünyada her şey kadının eseridir."

"Everything we see in the world is the work of women."

— Mustafa Kemal Atatürk, founder of
the modern-day Republic of Turkey

NOTE TO READERS

Turkey officially changed its name to Türkiye in June 2022 to accurately reflect the Turkish language. I deeply honor that decision and used that spelling in early drafts. However, as this book is a personal love story to a nation I knew as Turkey, I chose to use the version reflective of my heart language. I do not mean disrespect by this choice.

INTRODUCTION

IT IS DAWN and I am alone on a terrace strewn with Turkish carpets. I sit atop kilim pillows and watch the last of the hot air balloons sail past, silent but for the occasional blast of fire or a passenger's laughter cascading through the air. I have visited this town numerous times and even flown in one of those massive balloons, but I have never woken up early enough to watch the magical scene from the ground. As other early risers return to bed after the majority of the balloons make their descent, I linger with my Nescafé and thoughts.

This land has taken up residence inside of me, wooing me back over and over, always with a new lesson or revelation about life. It is the sanctuary where God and I speak plainly—my thin place where heaven and earth come close, where I pay attention and see more clearly.

On my way back to Turkey this trip, I routed through the sacred Isle of Iona, off the coast of Scotland. I had heard it was also a thin place, a popular pilgrimage, and so, after visiting friends in the north, I boarded a train from Inverness to Glasgow to Oban, took a ferry to the Isle of Mull, a bus across the island to Fionnphort, another ferry to Iona, and finally, walked a mile to my accommodation. The next morning, I hiked down to St. Columba's Bay, named for the famous saint who brought Christianity to Scotland in the sixth century. Hoping for a spiritual experience, I circled the labyrinth, searching for a glassy green tear-shaped stone symbolic of Columba's tears, and waited for a holy encounter that never came. Cold, wet, and hungry, I retraced my steps through ferns and sheep, past the abbey full of newly disembarked pilgrims, to warm up in my camping pod. I prayed and journaled and read the spiritual memoir about Iona I had packed for this very day, but heard nothing—received only silence. The famous thin place I spent so much effort to find was meaningless to me.

I lay awake that night, worried the ferry would be canceled (a very real possibility given the heat wave messing with train schedules and COVID-19 causing staff shortages) and that I'd be stuck and unable to make it to Turkey in time to lead the eight women arriving for our trip. And indeed, I awoke to a frantic camp host informing me that the ferry driver was sick and the routes were canceled for the day. The slim margin that existed between all of my subsequent connections shrank as I made my way to the port, hoping for an alternate solution. In the end, we were ferried back to Fionnphort in a small boat by Glen, a local fisherman, happy to help the stranded group of pilgrims gathered at the dock's end, looking forlornly at the water's edge.

I made it in time to Turkey, but instead of showing up full of the spiritual renewal I expected to receive on the sacred isle, I was primed for God to speak in the weary, needy state I always seem to find myself in when I'm in this place.

❧

My story in Turkey began as a recent college graduate, newly married, and longing for adventure and purpose. I was driven by principle: the largest unreached nation in the world needed me to bring them the gospel! One year became ten as I moved belongings, birthed babies, learned Turkish, and sowed seeds of sweat, tears, and long suffering.

Nothing was as I thought it should be: Language learning was fun until I plateaued and it felt impossible to reach a heart level proficiency; most Turks weren't actually spiritually interested; conflict with team leaders was difficult; life in a mega city was suffocating; I lived an undercover life as a Christian, constantly spinning different tales to different people; my husband was assaulted, depressed, and ready to leave years before I was; and after ten years, just weeks before we moved back home for good, our teammates were martyred. I returned to the United States fractured, traumatized, and so deeply, deeply weary. It took years to decompress.

Was it the place that wounded me? The organization with which I served? Or God himself? Bruised and battered, all of my stress and anxiety showed up in nightly dreams. Always located on the chaotic streets of Istanbul, I dreamt in Turkish, found myself negotiating fender benders, trying to order something from a shopkeeper, or any number of claustrophobic, culturally intense, language-dependent scenarios. Over time, however, something else began to show up in those dreams. In the midst of living under such stressful circumstances, we had experienced God in poignant ways. And, I longed for that again.

Eventually, that longing drew me back to Turkey. Time and again over these last two decades, for various projects and purposes, I've returned. Each time, I rediscover my faith. I hear something fresh from God. I see the life that wants to live in me a little more clearly. Questions I hadn't articulated or knew

I carried are answered. In this intense place, heaven and earth are near for me. It is my thin place. My Isle of Iona.

⌇

From the moment you deplane in Turkey, your senses are jarred. The airport smells of the same cleaning residue you'll notice in your hotel, and then, as soon as you exit, a waft of cigarette smoke engulfs you. No matter where you stay or how you get there, the crazy driving and traffic norms will leave you white knuckled. When you emerge from the vehicle at your destination, a whiff of coal assaults your nose as the Call to Prayer rattles your ears. You are in an exotic place.

If you sleep through the night, you awake to a breakfast feast of cucumbers and tomatoes, olives of all colors, fresh white cheeses, boiled eggs, an assortment of breads and jam, and instant coffee. Yes, the instant coffee may disappoint, but not for long: Shockingly, there are now over 700 Starbucks branches in Turkey, and you'll pass one soon enough. Mosque minarets dot the skyline, while produce sellers and trash collectors and tea delivery boys and chestnut roasters and carts selling corn on the cob and mopeds and taxis and stray cats all wrestle their way through the narrow cobblestone streets of this ancient city.

Most travelers to Turkey begin in Istanbul, and if you're a tourist, you'll probably head straight to the old town. Spend just one day behind the historic walls of Constantinople, in a fifth-century cistern beneath modern buildings, lost in a maze of shops in one of the bazaars, or shoulder to shoulder with people from around the world, and you will leave weary. Add to the historic and exotic a sensory overload: the colorful array of dried fruits and spices, hand woven carpets, painted ceramics, and women's headscarves; the smells of roasted lamb, cigarette smoke, and body odor; the sound of the Call to Prayer five times per day, honking taxi drivers, street vendors calling out their wares, and the steam engine ferries coming into port. By the end of Day One in Istanbul, your senses are jarred, and an unraveling begins. Nothing is as you thought it would be.

Rattled, exhausted, and desperate for a shower, you have a choice: You can be curious about where the jarring feels most unbearable—pay attention to how or why you are stirred—or raise your defenses—protect yourself from such vulnerability by critiquing and complaining. Oh, believe me, I'm well-versed in both.

Turkey, and more specifically Istanbul, always leaves me feeling weak and thin. And when I lean in and listen, I hear God in ways I don't in my everyday life. Sometimes it takes being stripped of our senses to see differently. The overwhelm of such a foreign place unlocks a younger space in our soul. We are not the confident, independent person who flew here but a day ago. The place becomes a metaphor. The experience becomes a crucible. If we choose curiosity, God has much to say to us here.

Fifteen years after we left Turkey, I began to facilitate a transformative experience for a small group of women. My insatiable hunger to uncover the stories of women who shaped this land sent me on a journey—searching history, archaeology, scripture, and legend to recover their fingerprints. Though I am not a historian in the strictly academic sense, I know what is true of the feminine soul. I combine all of this with my own experience to weave a timeless story. And now, eight strangers lend me their trust to guide them on a journey. As we traverse the country, moving from the congestion of Istanbul to the magical landscape of Cappadocia to the turquoise blue Aegean Coast, we follow the fingerprints of the women who shaped the places we visit. In exploring their stories in the very places they occurred, we allow our own to be reshaped.

In the sixth-century courtyard of a church-turned-mosque, we contemplate the political and spiritual influence of Empress Theodora, who literally left her signature on the columns inside. As modern women, have we not also navigated the muddy waters of a politicized faith? Or had to wield our power under the auspices of male authority?

In the sixteenth-century bathhouse commissioned by the sultan's favorite concubine, we consider the women of the neighborhood escaping domestic duties, exchanging gossip, and offering care to one another. How do we hold our own femininity, our hunger for mothering, or the lack of our own community of women?

We immerse ourselves in the textures of the ancient and current Anatolia, in the universal themes of femininity, and in the present company of our travel companions, and if we are listening, God speaks. The bathhouse exposes our body shame. The belly dancer evokes our objectification. The fourth-century female-led monastery calls into question our leadership and calling. The harem awakens our invisibility. Their fingerprints validate our experience. And our vulnerability provides space for the Spirit to move.

Unbeknownst to me, I had crafted a pilgrimage out of this place I love. As I allowed wise guides to deepen my understanding of sacred journeys, I found confirmation. One such sage, the Benedictine nun from Arkansas, Macrina Weiderkehr, wrote:

> A pilgrimage is a ritual journey with a hallowed purpose. Every step along the way has meaning. The pilgrim knows that the journey will be difficult and

that life-giving challenges will emerge. A pilgrimage is not a vacation; it is a transformational journey during which significant change takes place. New insights are given. Deeper understanding is attained. New and old places in the heart are visited. Blessings are received. Healing takes place. On return from pilgrimage, life is seen with different eyes. Nothing will ever be quite the same again.[1]

As one sojourner expressed to me after being back home for a few weeks, "I feel like the trip was just the beginning," as the *Lost Women of Turkey Pilgrimage* unearths how each of us longs to be found.

We begin in the sultan's harem of sixteenth-century Istanbul. We are literally behind bars. The day will hold a mix of emotions as we enter the world of the concubine. The Ottoman Empire shaped the streets we walk, and despite the cage the harem felt to us in the morning, the fingerprints of women are all over the landscape I lead us through. From there, we go back in time, each day jumping centuries all the way to the grand finale that will shock them all. Ottoman to Byzantine to Roman Empire. City to caves to sea. I will weave our way through the country and through history to tell a compelling feminine story: The further back we go, the more authority women have. By the time we walk the ancient road in Ephesus and wander through

---

1   Macrina Wiederkehr, *Behold Your Life: A Pilgrimage Through Your Memories* (Notre Dame, IN: Sorin Books, 2000), 11.

the frescoed walls and mosaic floors of wealthy Roman homes, Jesus' revolutionary view of women will feel palpable.

Could it be that what we most long for as women in the church existed in the first century? Long before buildings and hierarchy and councils, before women were slowly written out of leadership of this new faith, there was neither male nor female.

Slowly, we begin to embody the lost women who have shaped this land and our faith. We come to realize that we, too, have been lost. We make a pilgrimage to discover, uncover, and recover parts of us that have long been lost, unknown, unexplored, or invisible. We realize that we are the same, part of a global sisterhood that spans time and culture. It is no coincidence that by the time we're at the coast of the Aegean Sea, a spaciousness has widened in our souls. We breathe deeply the fresh, salty air and an expansive sense of our value as women. It has been the transformative journey Macrina Wiederkehr writes of. We are changed.

The sun has risen as the balloons disperse in all directions, and one glides over the terrace where I'm watching. The basket sails over me as I lie back on the pillows to video it, to prove to whomever cares how close it came. So close I feel I could reach out and grab hold of a corner, sail away above the fairy chimneys, like Aladdin on his magic carpet. Maybe the carpets beneath my feet will come alive and alight me through the sky. I'll grab my instant coffee and enjoy the sunrise with the rest of the balloonists. I'll sneak a view of the archaeological dig down the road; I'll be the first to notice a symbol in the recently uncovered mosaic floor. Wait a second. I'm lost in a daydream, drifting into the fiction version of this place I'm working on. Snapping out of the fantastical, I linger in the spiritual.

I feel the presence of God: in the warm breeze and sunbeams landing on my skin; in the rough woven wool of the carpets my shoeless feet rest upon or the pillows I am leaning against, the marvelous colors growing brighter as day begins; in the first quiet I've claimed on this women's trip; and in the memory of our conversation on this terrace from the night before. God has been at work in their stories, and as a result, in mine. I entered this trip asking questions, different from the ones I asked the last time I was here and different from the time before that. Twenty-five years ago, I followed a desire to live out my faith in this land. For a quarter of a century, it has remained an intricate part of the fabric of my story. I do not bring my questions to this place. I bring my questions to God and allow him to use this place to show me his answers. I imagine that this is what the Isle of Iona does for others. For me, it is this landscape, this history, and its sensory overload that creates the space for me to hear and see the Spirit.

As Thomas Merton writes, "The geographical pilgrimage is the symbolic acting out of an inner journey." And, as my co-leader Tracy says, "The journey is the destination."

You may not be able to join me among the exotic streets of Istanbul or in the honeycomb tunnels of Cappadocia or the mosaic floors of Ephesus, but let me invite you to the next best thing: into a journey of discovering more of what you, too, have lost. Perhaps you'll recover her in the twists and turns of the storied travel I'm about to take you on.

Recipes and reflection questions are provided at the end of each chapter for you to gather with friends and consider where the stories intersect with your own.

MAP

EUROPE
THE BLACK SEA
ISTANBUL
SEA OF MARMARA
ANKARA (GALATIA)
KUZEY ANDAOLU MTNS
MT. ARARAT
CAPPADOCIA
AVANOS
KAYSERI
GÖREME
EPHESUS
LAODICEA
KONYA (ICONIUM)
ÇATALHÖYÜK
TAURUS MTNS
THE AEGEAN SEA
THE MEDITERRANEAN SEA
ANTIOCH
SYRIA

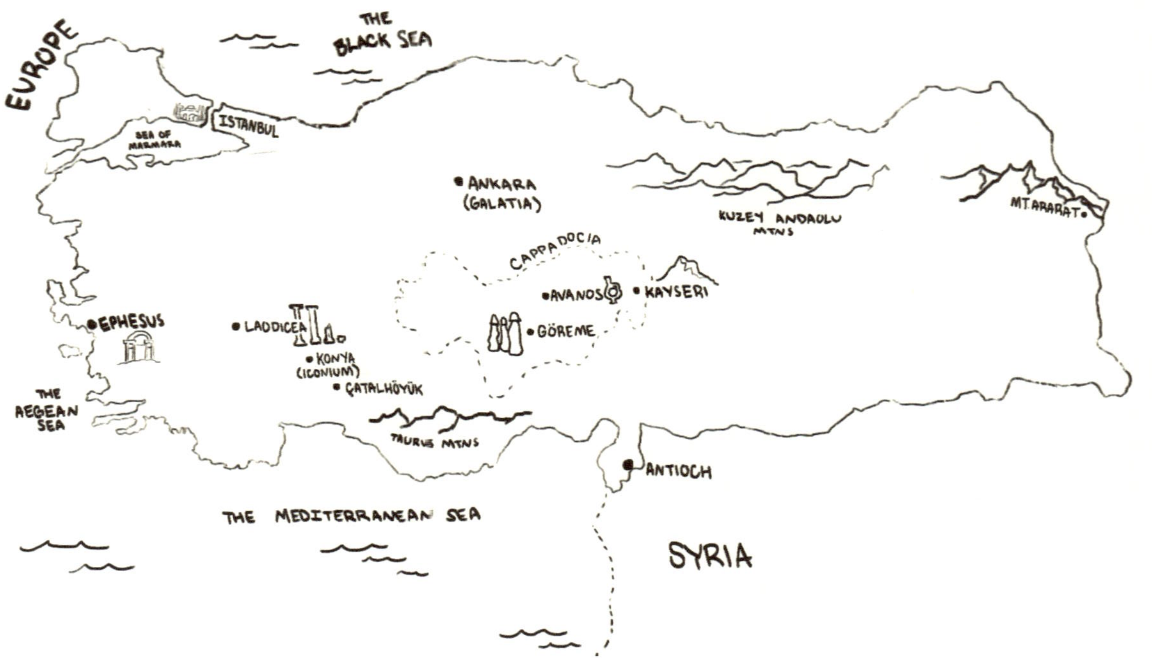

PART 1

ISTANBUL: BEHIND LATTICED WINDOWS

16TH-17TH CENTURIES

MACRINA TELLS US that the pilgrim knows the journey will be difficult, but that life-giving challenges will emerge along the way. Those who traverse the Camino de Santiago or the Highland Way experience the necessary physical stripping through the days-long trek and the fierce elements. These pilgrims know what awaits and prepare by working in new boots, taking long hikes, and buying the right gear. They anticipate sore feet and chilled bones; they know this is part of the process of a transformational journey. If one is properly prepared, Istanbul also provides this necessary aspect of pilgrimage.

The city is bursting with tourists, refugees, villagers, and a growing middle class. Millions of people fill every crevice. It is noisy all the time, and physically distressing. People are rarely in public alone, and so there is no privacy, no serenity. Even parks are crowded with groups of friends and large families. It is worse in the oldest section of ancient Constantinople, where we must go to find the stories of our lost women. People jostle our bodies, and personal space is nonexistent. And, because there are treasures around every corner, we must walk thousands of steps a day, on cobblestone, up and down the seven hills upon which

13

the city is built. Istanbul is an embodied, physically demanding beginning to the pilgrimage, and entirely intentional.

Pilgrimage is moving with a "sacred purpose, a sacred intention." As much as we craft the beginning of our trip to strip away many of the protective strategies we often employ and succeed with, we also purposefully start in a time period that comes closest to our own. The Ottoman Empire's one-hundred-year reign of women, known as the Sultanate of Women (during the sixteenth to seventeenth centuries), was full of paradox. The women of the harem were slaves, existing for the pleasure of the sultan, and yet, for the ones who became favorites, simultaneously the wealthiest and most powerful women in the empire. They were both trapped behind guarded quarters and also some of the most influential women of the century. It begs the question: Where do women still experience a similar enslavement? Where do women still feel like they serve the pleasure of men? And what are the wealthy and influential women of our time doing with their power?

After the brutality and beauty of Istanbul finishes her assault on our senses through the shock of the harem and the sensual Turkish bath and the last evening prayer, as we sit between the Hagia Sophia Church and the Blue Mosque, there is a deeper layer of experiencing this place with other women. Nowhere are our projections and personas more viciously activated than in the company of other women. Hagar and Sarah may help us understand envy as we sit between the two symbols of their legacy (Christianity and Islam), but they do little to alleviate its effects, which are on full display by the end of two days in Istanbul. Conversation over slow al fresco dinners or while walking between ancient monuments often surfaces comparisons, anxiety, and shame—well-known companions of all women.

It is all a part of stage one of the journey—our Turkish version of the Camino or the Scottish Highlands. We have to start in Istanbul, and the pilgrim needs to be prepared, for the process requires both a level of physical resilience and emotional vulnerability to begin well.

As a foreign resident, I treated Istanbul like a colonizer, a place and a people to conquer and change. Without respect for the journey she could lead me on, I viewed her as a destination to reach. Without mutual respect, she chewed me up and spat me out. My husband, who leads Highland Way pilgrimages for men, tells me how similar it is in the Scottish mountains—the rugged crags, foggy days, and ferocious wind against your chest constantly demand respect. When we yield, "new insights are given. Deeper understanding is attained." The initial stage of pilgrimage requires stripping away our defenses. Pilgrims do not yet know they, too, are lost women. With attention, intention, and precision, we begin.

HAREM

I HAVE TRIED to watch the Turkish soap opera about the sixteenth-century reign of Süleyman the Magnificent. I watch with subtitles and try to get past the dramatic catfights between the harem concubines because the history is helpful, but it is difficult to watch. Turkish television has undergone significant improvement since the airing of *Magnificent Century* in 2011. Now, the industry rivals Hollywood and Bollywood and is rumored to be significantly supported by the government. President Erdoğan is said to visit the sets of historical films that promote the glorious rule of the Islamic Ottoman Empire.[2] Their stories are what soap operas are made of, so I guess *Magnificent Century* has captured it well.

Visitors to the former capital of the Ottoman Empire can visit not one, but two palace harems, and allow their imaginations to

---

2   As of this publication, Recep Tayyip Erdoğan has been the President of the Republic of Turkey since 2014. The 12th president of the Republic, Wikipedia says the following: "Coming from an Islamist background and promoting socially conservative policies, Turkey has experienced increasing authoritarianism, democratic backsliding and suppression of dissent under Erdoğan's rule."

wander. In the older of the two palaces, Topkapı, built in 1459 by Mehmed the Conqueror of Constantinople, the harem has been restored. Topkapı was home to the sultans, their families, and their administrative center for over 400 years until construction on the modern and Europeanized Dolmabahçe Palace in 1856 made it their new home.[3] Topkapı's harem was added by Süleyman when he moved his family into it in the 1500s. At its height, over 4,000 people lived and worked within these palace walls.

You may be picturing a luxurious brothel full of sex slaves and sensuality. Perhaps you've heard that there were hundreds of women housed in the harem and that only the sultan had access to them. In actuality, that is an oversimplification of the micro-society that existed in this part of the palace and is too dismissive of the power some of these women wielded. Indeed, as mentioned before, an entire century is thought to have been held together by the few women who had the most influence over the sultans.

But you are not wrong to picture hundreds of women. And they were indeed all slaves. Ottomans believed they could not enslave fellow Muslims, and so, as they expanded their borders, they enslaved Christians and Jews, selling young women as concubines to the harem and young boys to the military. The girls were chosen by the sultan's mother, the most powerful and wealthiest woman in the empire. They entered the harem to begin their education in Persian, poetry, embroidery, social

---

3   A sultan was a king of the Ottoman Empire. The last sultan went into exile in 1922 when the Ottoman Empire was dissolved by the Grand Assembly of Turkey. The Republic of Turkey was formed in 1923 with Mustafa Kemal Atatürk, its first president.

etiquette, dance, and all the skills necessary to become a favorite of the sultan one day.

§

We gather in the harem as I share insights about the power dynamics and complexity of these women. There are wives, mothers, and favorite concubines whose names history remembers only because of their association with sultans. They used their allowance to commission many of the bazaars, hamams, and mosques still standing today. I have tried to learn and remember as many of the sordid facts as I can and begin to describe the litany of both their nefarious and benevolent actions.

We walk through the eunuchs' quarters, those castrated male slaves charged with protecting the harem, the only males allowed in the harem aside from the sultan himself. We see the sleeping platforms for the majority of the concubines, the hundreds who lived here and merely served the favorites, never themselves sent to the sultan. Contrary to popular belief, the concubines were not only here for the sultan. There was a mistress for everything: coffee, sherbet, jewels, dress, laundry.

On our first pilgrimage, my daughter is with me. Sixteen and, though not her first time here, her first time registering it all. She quietly moves through the rooms and corridors, taking photos of the latticed windows through which a concubine might have viewed foreign visitors or palace intrigue. Our tour guide tried to spin a pretty picture: *The girls in the harem were educated, well fed, well dressed, and lived a much better life than if they had remained in their village, or worse, been slaughtered like the older women would have been as the Ottoman Empire expanded.* But those windows. That hallway to the sultan's room. The thought of the girl who was sent only once. Wait. Is that better or worse? We're feeling confused. This place is so strange. Are we rooting for their favor or dismissal? I always feel an odd mix of repulsion by the system and pride in the girls who succeed in it. As we emerge from the maze of rooms and buildings to regroup and process, my daughter is still lost in thought.

To lead this trip, I have amassed 100 years of history of powerful women. Women who wielded their influence for good and used it for evil. Women who harmed each other in their strategic maneuvering to survive. I wonder aloud how we, too, wield our influence and ask if perhaps we have harmed another woman in our own power grab. The women of our group are talking, mostly unable to wrap their minds around the objectification and sexualization the harem girls faced.

But then my daughter speaks, the glisten of a tear in her eye. She is shaken by the story of Sultan Ibrahim I, the raving mad ruler of 1640, who, after hearing of an affair occurring in the harem, had 278 concubines drowned in the Bosphorus. "What about them?" she asks. "Who were they? Do we even know their names? *Those* are the ones I relate to. The invisible ones. The hundreds of women whose names we'll never know. Because that's me—that's a story I get."

And it occurs to me that even now we're missing their fingerprints. Despite how hard I've worked to pull out of the brick and mortar stories of Hürrem, Nurbanu, Safiye, Turhan, Kösem, and how I've learned who commissioned each building we pass, there are still so many women who shaped this place and its history that I will never know. My daughter is right. They are still invisible.

Except *she* relates to them. My Gen Z daughter sees them. She knows what it is to feel unseen; not to be chosen, whether you want to be or not; to be dismissed and disregarded by males who value themselves above women. Her tears were for the 278 lying at the bottom of the Bosphorus Strait. Mine are for a girl whose tenderness and self-reflection honor the plight of women throughout time. She saw them. And perhaps that is enough to make them visible again.

Long before I realized that Junia's name had been masculinized or noticed the presence of women like Susanna and Joanna traveling with Jesus, I had Esther and Ruth.[4] At least I had them. They were the sole heroines in our Bible studies, as leaders gave PG explanations of what it meant that Ruth "lay at Boaz's feet and uncovered them," or that Esther saved her people through "generous hospitality." The most exotic and erotic place a Westerner sees in Istanbul plays a prominent role in scripture, at least for women, for it is where women are often found.[5] But we did not discuss the harem in our Bible studies.

After years of anti-trafficking work, I used to view the harem as a brothel, full of sex slaves, captured and sold for the sultan's pleasure. When I entered the harem bath, I imagined Esther's beauty treatments and preparations for the first night the king would summon her. In the concubines' quarters, I pictured

---

4   Though widely understood to be female in early historical commentary, Junia was changed to Junias in the 13th century and remained male until 2011 (NIV) and 2020 (NASB) when Romans 16:7 was revised to reflect her gender.

5   A brief list of the women named in the Old Testament who are one of many wives: Sarah, Hagar, Keturah, Leah, Rachel, Bilhah, Zilpah, Michal, Abigail, Bathsheba, Solomon's wives and concubines, Rizpah, Maacah, Esther, Vashti, and many unnamed wives/concubines of kings.

the sultan walking by, making his evening choice. Through the years, I've developed a more complicated understanding of the nature of trauma, survival skills, and human nature. Now I walk through the harem looking for nuance: The women here were young, innocent girls who became cunningly powerful women to survive.

Just outside of the entrance to the harem is the sultan's throne room, where a large, cushioned divan sits low against the wall in the center of the room.[6] Lining the other three walls are low cushioned benches where advisors sat, and together, they would receive foreign dignitaries. The entire room is tiled floor to ceiling, and gold-plated iron bars cover the windows. It's an ornate room, but one I rarely gave much attention to until I studied the Sultanate of Women: the 100 years in which the wives and mothers and grandmothers of the sultans were said to have held the empire together.

About six feet above the sultan's divan is a rectangular window, entirely covered by the same gold-plated iron bars and a latticed sheath behind it. Imagine my surprise when I realized the sultan's throne room was connected to the harem and the women could observe government proceedings from within the secluded corridor behind. While there was no way to see inside the harem from this window, the women on the other side could see out, and they could certainly hear… and whisper. And, in the early years of the seventeenth century, when some sultans were as young as seven, their mothers or, in one case, their grandmother, would whisper advice and instructions from above.

---

6   A divan was a long, low-to-the-ground cushion serving as a couch of sorts. It also served as a throne. The main road through the Sultanahmet neighborhood, where we spend our time in Istanbul, is called "Divan Yolu" or "The Road to the Throne."

❧

I stand at the base of the latticed window, shaken. I am not thinking about Kösem, who stood at that window through five sultans in her years at Topkapı. I'm not considering any of the women who may have had good ideas, disputes, or solutions to the affairs of state they overheard. No, I'm standing there looking up, feeling very much like the girl behind the lattice. It's my second pilgrimage, and it holds a different theme for me than the first. This time, I'm in the midst of a major role transition with my husband and our business, and I find my body is stirred by that window.

For years, I have been the invisible voice offering counsel to the man on the divan of not one, but two organizations that he started and leads. I love them and him dearly and have treasured my involvement, mostly feeling like my input is valued and wanted. But over the last couple of years, as the organizations have both grown, my secret counsel has caused some confusion and hurt. It has felt incongruent with who I am and how our marriage works. To be honest, we are both tired of that damn window—me for being hidden, him for having to sit in that seat. Prior to this trip, we announced a decision we had mulled over for months: He would step out of the role of CEO of our business and give it to me.

We've never doubted my strength; we never held traditional or patriarchal beliefs we had to overcome. But we're not dumb. We understood the structures in which we operated and learned how to adapt to them for our benefit. Because of our marriage, it worked until it just started to be weird. Times had changed in the nearly three decades we had been together. We didn't need to play any sort of role anymore. We didn't need him to be the representative of "The Brunos." And besides, I was starting to feel suffocated behind the lattice.

❧

I wonder if Hürrem, whose reign began the Sultanate of Women, felt similarly in her marriage to Süleyman. Theirs was a legendary sixteenth-century romance between the sultan and the feisty, red-headed Anastasia, captured from Ukraine in a raid and given the Persian name "laughing one." The one whom Süleyman fell in love with, breaking Ottoman tradition to not only father more than one son with her, but also marry and make her a legal wife.[7] She was known to have had diplomatic influence, especially during his long absences in war. Was theirs a relationship of equals? Did they whisper strategies alongside their famous poetic love letters?

Outside the palace, just across from the great Hagia Sophia Church, Hürrem built a public bathhouse so that pilgrims (to the then mosque) could bathe. Not far from there, she built a large complex that included a mosque, a school, a soup kitchen, a hostel, and a hospital. Modeling the philanthropy common among the wealthy in Byzantium, the sultan's wives

---

7   The Ottoman tradition of sultans not marrying was due to a number of reasons. Concubines were slaves, not princesses who came from wealthy, influential families demanding something in return. Concubines prevented political ties that other kingdoms demanded, as in the royal marriages in Europe and England. The One Concubine, One Son rule also prevented women from gaining too much power. Sons and their mothers were sent to remote regions for the boys to learn to rule on a smaller scale and to prevent them from seizing the throne before the sultan's death. Successive rule came through whichever son claimed the throne first and then killed all his brothers.

and mothers were some of the most affluent and most charitable women in the world. The most common way to showcase their power and influence, as well as their favor with the sultan, was to commission buildings for the community. Today, Istanbul's historic skyline is marked by the legacy of these benefactresses.

Hürrem's son, Selim, succeeded his father to the throne and legally married his favorite concubine, Nurbanu, a beautiful and intelligent Venetian. She became extremely powerful, advising Selim's Grand Vizier, who essentially ruled the empire at the time, and continued to influence her son, Murad, when he succeeded to the throne (which she shrewdly ensured by keeping Selim's dead body on ice to give Murad time to get to Istanbul and claim the throne over his brothers). Murad created an official title for his beloved mother, *Valide Sultan* (mother of the sultan), which guaranteed her and future Valide Sultans even more authority. She is responsible for the construction of my favorite Turkish bath, Çemberlitaş Hamamı.

Murad's favorite concubine was Safiye, who allegedly wrote letters to Queen Elizabeth and moved about the city incognito. It wasn't until Murad died and Safiye's son, Mehmed, became sultan, that her role as Valide Sultan afforded her significant influence.[8] She received three times as much money as her son, making her the highest-paid person in the empire. Her son sought her advice, as did other leaders. She started construction on the "New Valide Sultan Mosque," now known simply as the Yeni (New) Mosque. I smile every single time I hear that name, *new*, since it was built in the 1600s and still looms over

---

8   A favorite concubine in the Ottoman Empire meant she held extraordinary power and influence over the sultan and was given privilege and wealth above any other in the harem, except his mother.

the Eminönü port. Mehmed favored the concubine Turhan, and she oversaw the completion of the New Mosque, its related charitable services, and the nearby Egyptian Spice Bazaar, which funded both projects.

For one hundred years, the strongest women led the empire from behind that latticed window. From captured village girls to the wealthiest women in the largest empire in the world, these women learned to bend and yield. They learned to play the role for their benefit. They may have thrived. For sure, they survived.

It's all so exotic. Eunuchs and marble baths and latticed windows. Conspiracy and murder, poison and drownings, and bodies on ice. Palace intrigue made for soap operas. It can feel completely strange, foreign, even barbaric.

I've moved on from the throne room with the divan and the latticed window. Familiar with the tiled rooms laid out like a maze, I meander through the harem, distracted by how much I've located myself in this place on this trip. The Valide Sultan's rooms have been recently renovated and are open for the first time in a long time. They are right next door to the sultan's rooms. A clearer picture of her role there is not.

There is much that creates distance and that is hard to relate to, but I can't shake the sameness. The way women have navigated structures of power, both masculine and feminine, over time; the way women have wielded hidden influence; the way women have led without position. I'm returning to my own official title, but all of that? *That* I know in my bones. My body knows it to be true, and it shook beneath the window in resonance.

Where have you wielded a hidden influence or known what it is to be behind a latticed window? Like me, has there been a metaphorical sultan on the divan of your life? Where are you now?

OTTOMAN FAMILY TREE

SULTANATE OF WOMEN

Sultan	Consort or Mother	Son Who Took the Throne
Suleiman the Magnificent (r. 1520–1566)	Hürrem Sultan (wife)	Selim II
Selim II (r. 1566–1574)	Nurbanu Sultan (wife or concubine)	Murad III
Murad III (r. 1574–1595)	Safiye Sultan (consort)	Mehmed III
Mehmed III (r. 1595–1603)	Handan Sultan (consort)	Ahmed I
Ahmed I (r. 1603–1617)	Kösem Sultan (Haseki & later Valide Sultan)	Murad IV
Murad IV (r. 1623–1640)	Kösem Sultan (mother)	—
Ibrahim I (r. 1640–1648)	Kösem Sultan (mother)	Mehmed IV
Mehmed IV (r. 1648–1687)	Turhan Hatice Sultan (mother, Kösem's rival)	—

PERDE PILAV

My favorite Turkish rice dish means "veiled rice" because tucked inside multiple layers of buttery pastry is a savory mix of chicken, rice, currants, and pine nuts. This would typically be served at a wedding feast as a symbol of a new home and fertility. The slave girls of the harem faced a different reality as they entered their new living situation, and the symbolism is unmistakable: their new home was a veiled existence. This is a fitting dish for discussing the harem in your life.

1. The key to Turkish rice is butter. Sauté 1 diced onion in several tablespoons of butter. When softened, add 2 cups of rinsed rice and fry. When crisp, add 4 cups of chicken broth and cover the pan.

2. In another pan, add 2 cups of shredded cooked chicken, along with cinnamon, nutmeg, salt, and pepper to taste. Add softened currants (or raisins) and toasted pine nuts.

3. Mix rice and chicken.

4. In a large casserole dish (round or oval works best), spread melted butter on the bottom and place blanched almonds in a design

of your choosing. Place one sheet of phyllo pastry on top, draping the rest up over the sides. Continue to spread butter and lay one sheet of dough until you've used one sleeve of the packet. Into the dish, press the rice mixture and then fold the phyllo sheets over the top. You may need to add a few more sheets in the same fashion to cover everything.

5. Cook until browned, then cool slightly and flip over onto a serving plate. The lovely almond design should be on top, and you can cut into it like a cake.

6. Alternatively, if you have 5-inch ramekins, you can make individual versions of these.

LOKUM

THE ADDICTIVE SWEET that tempts Edward to betray his brother and sisters and follow the White Witch was coined "Turkish Delight" by a European in the early nineteenth century after bringing back a stash from Istanbul and sharing it with his friends at home. In Turkey, it's called lokum, and it is traditionally served alongside a small demitasse cup of Turkish coffee. All over the country, you can purchase cellophane-wrapped boxes of the desert, much like you can saltwater taffy or assorted chocolates in the States. To be honest, I never really liked the chewy, fruity squares covered in powdered sugar. Not until I tasted the pistachio variety from the original creator of lokum, Ali Muhiddin Haci Bekir.

In 1777, Ali Muhiddin opened up a shop near the New Mosque, down the hill from the palace. Confections were relatively new to Turkey, and Ali was a master of them. He was also a traveler, making a pilgrimage to Mecca, earning the title Haci (from the Arabic Hajj or *one who made the pilgrimage*), as well as to Europe, where he learned about cornstarch. Swapping cornstarch for flour in his candy produced lokum, and by 1820, the sultan himself had so fallen in love with this sugary goodness that he named Ali the Chief Confectioner of the palace. Ali went on to compete in fairs in Europe, winning medals and spreading the fame of Turkish lokum.

The business grew and stayed in the family. Today, 250 years later, it remains the oldest family-run business in Turkey, having been managed by women for the last three generations. Their classic variety, pistachio, is my favorite; the combination of salty and sweet is perfect.

The original shop is on a busy street that connects the tram stop to the Egyptian Spice Bazaar. I lead the women down the sidewalk, wondering why I'm not carrying one of those umbrellas or bandana-wrapped poles to lead the ones who walk too fast, the ones who walk quite slow, the ones who get cut off because they're too polite, the ones not paying attention, the ones wishing they were in charge. When I see the shop, I pause and let everyone catch up. It's a surprise. I'm going to buy a box of my favorite Turkish Delight for them to try, but first, they need to hear that the business that started in this very storefront in 1777 has been run by women for the last few generations and is currently managed by sixth generation Leyla Celalyan.

There are many strong women in modern Turkey. Turks elected a female Prime Minister in the 1990s, 46% of Turkish academics are female, and the rate of female college graduates is growing. And yet, I'm still moved by the visible, tangible proof of female ownership and business acumen in a country where the outward-facing service industry is so male-dominated. Celalyan herself says, "Haci Bekir is such a masculine and traditional name but when you look at the company, it's been mostly females at the head."[9]

The women in our group all agree that this version of lokum is worlds away from what they've tried in imported boxes in America. If this is what caused Edward to change his loyalty to the White Witch, we understand. However, our taste buds may be a little biased towards a female-owned brand. It's a double delight to enjoy a three-century legacy of ingenuity. We'll keep dipping into that box for days; the endless supply of little white squares leaves sugar dust on all we touch. But that's what we do, isn't it? We leave behind our fingerprints. I'll thank Leyla someday.

We make our way up the hill behind the Egyptian Spice Bazaar and enter a world frozen in time, with streets full of fabric and applique shops for bridal gowns and dishware, and linen shops for dowries.[10] This is ancient Istanbul, an area of town where a more traditional Turkish woman still does her shopping. Stacks of spices, dried fruit and nuts, fresh cheeses straight from the village, candies of all varieties, baklavas and honeyed sweets of all shapes, fish that would scare a baby, and olives of every shade of green beckon from the left and right. The scent of freshly

---

9   Jasmine Alimin, "The Story of a 240-Year-Old Sweet Shop That Makes Turkish Delights Fit for a King," *CNA Luxury*, February 2, 2020, https://cnaluxury.channelnewsasia.com/remarkableliving/turkish-delight-heritage-shop-istanbul-173781.

10 This bazaar was originally called the "Valide Bazaar" or "Mother of the Sultan Bazaar" and came to be known as the Egyptian Spice Bazaar in the mid-19th century because the spices were largely imported (and highly taxed) from Egypt.

ground Turkish coffee fills one street, only to be surpassed by the aroma of roasting lamb around the next corner. The more conservative district is a little uncomfortable for our group, as we push past women in headscarves and long coats, as well as even more conservatively dressed Middle Eastern tourists who have come to Istanbul on a shopping spree.

As we walk further up the hill, the little shops give way to tables topped with piles of jeans, soccer jerseys, and knockoff Nike shoes and Louis Vuitton bags. If we were to keep going, we would eventually find ourselves at the mouth of the Grand Bazaar, an older version of the Egyptian Spice Bazaar. The Grand Bazaar had been a thriving commerce center since 1455, but the empire was growing. Another bazaar was built in 1651 not far away, and it is to *this* bazaar, built by the woman at the center of this century, that I lead my group after we try Turkish Delight: Büyük Valide Han.

Like so many historic buildings still standing in Istanbul, if you don't know what you're looking for, you can easily miss it. This particular bazaar is situated right off a street that narrows to about six feet in width. Blackened stones frame an arched stairwell that leads to darkened corridors and alcoved work-stations, where a welder, a seamstress, and various craftsmen still work in tiny spaces lit by single bulbs. At the end of the second corridor is a coffee shop with a small balcony view of the Golden Horn. But at the other end, further into the darkness of underuse, the Ottoman wall is built into a Byzantine tower. It is here that my curiosity rests. Why would the woman who com-missioned the building, Kösem Sultan, attach it to this tower?

❧

In my third year in college, I moved into a big old house on the corner of Foster and Sherman Avenue, three doors down from my fiancé. There were nine of us girls in the "eight-bedroom," two-bath house. Karen's room was so small she couldn't fit a bed, but there was an odd hole in the wall, just at eye level, big enough for a twin mattress. Amber had two rooms on the third floor: one large enough for her clothes and one just big enough for a mattress on the floor. Four girls shared two rooms, and I cannot remember why I had my very own, rather large room with a stained glass closet with built-in shelves. Did we draw straws? Have I purposefully forgotten how I got it? We were busy juniors and seniors and not all close, so there were few all-house hangouts. Embarrassingly, I can't even remember the name of one roommate. Besides, I was planning a wedding, and the groom was living a few steps away. I was rarely at 2000 Sherman Avenue.

But whenever I picture the harem, I remember the dynamics within my college house where nine girls shared two small bathrooms and one kitchen. I remember the pile of dishes in the sink and hair in the drain. I remember the nauseating smell of too many beauty products and the relief of having my own tidy space in which to hide. We never had a house cleaner, and therefore, I'm not sure any of the public spaces were ever cleaned. I guess it's not very similar to the harem at all. There were no eunuchs, no luxurious bathing experiences, no chef, and no Valide Sultan in charge. Although sometimes, I wished for one.

The harem which Kösem commanded might have felt equally crowded. By the time fifteen-year-old Anastasia was taken from her Greek Father-Priest's home and sold to Sultan Ahmed's mother, Handan, in 1603, the harem was a city unto itself. Just two sultans before, in 1574, Murad III had increased the harem from 150 to 600 concubines. Women had titles such as Mistress of Laundry, Mistress of Sherbet, and Mistress of Jewels. Murad loved the concubine Safiye best, which, in harem politics, threatened his mother, Nurbanu, who actually tried to weaken Safiye's influence by distracting her son with other concubines. Eventually, it was his sister, colluding with their mother, who succeeded in diluting Safiye's influence, as Murad III ultimately fathered twenty-seven girls and twenty boys with the distracting concubines!

Mehmed was the son who became heir to Murad III, and to secure his crown, he immediately had his nineteen brothers murdered, enraging the city. It was then Mehmed's son, Ahmed, to whom Anastasia was given after she was prophetically renamed Kösem, meaning "leader of the herd." Aptly named, for soon after becoming Ahmed's favorite, his mother Handan died, leaving no Valide Sultan to stand in Kösem's way. She quickly became the most powerful woman in the Ottoman Empire. They had four daughters and five sons before Ahmed died of typhus in 1617 at the age of twenty-seven. Thus began Kösem's power play that lasted thirty-four years.

If that all feels confusing, I'm not sure you'll follow what happens next. It reads like the best of soap operas, and it's hard to differentiate what is legend and what is truth. Take from it the themes the legend tells us, and don't worry about the particularities. The legend is how people made meaning from their reality.

⁂

Up until now, succession had come through fratricide: the son who claimed the throne first subsequently killed all other brothers to secure his reign. But when Ahmed became sultan at age thirteen, he did not kill his brother Mustafa, ending this practice. So, when Ahmed died with only young children and a surviving brother, for the first time succession went to the eldest male. However, Mustafa held the title for just ninety-six days before he was deemed mentally unfit and deposed. Another of Ahmed's sons from a different concubine, Osman, became sultan at the age of fourteen and ruled for four years. While working to secure the eastern border, Osman failed in Poland and blamed the Janissaries, punishing them by reducing their numbers, closing their coffeehouses, and threatening to create a whole new army.[11] This angered them so much that they snuck in and strangled Osman, which put Mustafa back on the throne because Ahmed's other sons were still so young.

Mustafa was on the throne for one year before being deposed again, but allowed to live in what was literally called the "Male Cage" on the palace grounds: a small, secured cottage of sorts. Kösem and her children had been living in another palace, but returned to Topkapı with eleven-year-old Murad, playing the role of regent and attending cabinet meetings from behind a screen.[12] She rather liked her influence, and as Murad

---

11 Janissaries were similar to the Secret Service. They were the sultan's private soldiers and bodyguards, seen as an elite branch of the military. They were Christian boys who had been taken from their homes in the Balkans (like the girls who ended up as concubines in the harem) and raised to become soldiers. The coffeehouse was like an American Legion Hall or USO Lounge: a communal gathering place for brothers in arms.

12 A regent is a person who rules in place of the appointed ruler (sultan) when the ruler is too young, incapacitated, or otherwise unfit or unable to rule. Kösem played regent multiple times to her sons and grandsons.

aged, she attempted to keep him otherwise preoccupied with concubines. He picked up on her ploys and tried to get rid of her. To maintain her advantage, Kösem warned Murad of a plot to kill *him*, which endeared him to her and bought her time. Murad, an insecure guy now, instead issued an order to kill his brothers out of fear that they were the ones behind the murder plot (just when the empire hoped this practice had ended).

Kösem begged her son to at least spare his crazy little brother İbrahim, which he agreed to do for a while, but after she learned of his plans to kill İbrahim after all, Murad was found poisoned to death in his bed. Now, Kösem found herself steering the empire through another son, the crazy and impotent İbrahim, known as "The Mad." This guy was truly not well. After several remedies and attempts to cure him of impotence, he not only fathered a child, but became a sex addict. I'll spare you from the deviant behavior history has recorded, but you might recall that this was the sultan who drowned 278 women after hearing of an affair in the harem. Had Kösem's influence on her son waned? Surely she would not have condoned such an atrocity!

İbrahim was strangled soon after the drowning incident, and his son (he ended up with eighteen children), Mehmed IV, became heir. Again, too young to rule, Kösem played regent, despite his mother Turhan's presence, because she was also too young to overrule Kösem. As Turhan grew in her own influence, she began to resent Kösem's power. And so, Kösem plotted the overthrow of her grandson for another with a weaker mother and supposedly gave poisoned sherbet to the cook to give to Mehmed. (Yes, Kösem was a mass murderer if these stories are all true.) But, in the layered palace intrigue, a servant tipped off Turhan, and she got to Kösem first, who was found strangled and robbed in her quarters.

The city spontaneously erupted into three days of mourning over Kösem's death. I've told you the ways Kösem manipulated and murdered to maintain her power, but the people loved her. She freed her slaves after three years of working for her and gave the women dowries to marry. She supposedly dressed up in a disguise to personally go to the debtors' prison and arrange for their release. Despite how she wielded her power and kept her influence, she managed to hold the empire together during a tumultuous period of leadership. Her death in 1651 marked the end of 100 years of the wives, mothers, and grandmothers of sultans leading from behind latticed windows, whispering through screens, and holding the ear of the men who bore the title. The Sultanate of Women came to an end with Kösem's death.

We find the bazaar tucked away off the busy street and walk through the dark corridors of the building Kösem commissioned: the Büyük Valide Han.[13] In a 400-year-old structure bearing her name, I wonder at her choice of location. Why connect this marketplace-inn to the Byzantine tower in the corner? It was said that her treasures were stored there, which, given the palace politics, was probably a wise move on her part. But could there have been another reason she commissioned this building?

We walk the darkened corridors of the han and, as we catch our breath from the long walk uphill in the heat of the day, the weight of the complexity of power and influence sits heavily on

---

13 A han is a large inn or caravansaray. They were built to house camels and traveling merchants in stalls on the bottom level and serve as a market on upper levels. This one is translated, "The Grandmother of the Sultan's Inn."

my soul. We may not be able to understand the power dynamics and relational intrigue of the sultan's harem or mother, but we, too, have known power plays. We have manipulated, haven't we? We have been maneuvered. We are aware of the world of influence, yet we both shun it and consume it. We live in a culture that idolizes the charismatic leader, and when they fail us, our only recourse seems to be to cancel them. As women, we are as complex as Kösem. Hopefully not poisoning our sons and grandsons while being a benefactor to the poor, but inconsistent, hypocritical, supportive, and ambivalent all the same.

Legend tells us that she held the empire together, yet we know power is a heavy burden to bear. I've regretted decisions I made in positions of power. I'm embarrassed by the control I clung to. I am Kösem, as are you. And I am Leyla, the family business owner, holding together a different sort of empire with its own complexity, committed to a family legacy of her own.

It's like that with pistachio lokum: a little bit of sweet and a little bit of salt.

> *Where have you regretted decisions made in positions of power? How have you known the human games we play for dominance in groups of women? Where is your glory? Where is your depravity? What would it look like to grieve and celebrate both sides of yourself?*

LOKUM

I've described the origin of Turkish Delight and the best source of the real thing. You can always pick some up at your nearest Middle Eastern grocer, and, I can't believe this, but you can also buy Haci Bekir Pistachio Lokum on Amazon! I've tried making it myself, and it's challenging. Mine ended up in a blob shape rather than a cute cube. But if you're adventurous, here is a recipe I suggest trying: [14]

1. Line an 8"x8" pan with plastic wrap.

2. Mix ¼ cup of cornstarch with ¼ cup of powdered sugar, and use a little to dust the pan.

3. Heat 3 ½ cups sugar, 1 ⅔ cups water, and the juice of 1 lemon in a pan, but do not boil.

4. In a separate bowl, combine ⅔ cups of cornstarch with 100 ml of cold water. Add this to the sugar syrup.

5. Gradually add three tablespoons of powdered gelatin to the syrup mixture, being careful to remove all lumps.

6. Bring to a boil, then reduce the heat to low and continue cooking for 20 more minutes, whisking constantly. You're looking for it to become a pale yellow color.

---

14 "Basic Rahat Lokum", *Taste Atlas*. https://www.tasteatlas.com/lokum/recipe/basic-rahat-lokum.

7. Either add rose water or pistachios. Pour the mixture into the pan and let it cool overnight in a cool place.

8. The next day, dust a surface with the remaining mix from step #2 and plop the lokum on top. Cut into cubes and serve!

HAMAM

THERE IS A place I like to go that makes me feel brave and beautiful.

From the congested street corner, you might miss it. If you didn't know it was there, you would most likely be watching for the tram or checking from which direction the long line of honking taxis would emerge first. You might be distracted by the guy squeezing fresh pomegranates or the one shaving lamb döner on the other side of the double doors leading down to marble steps. And of course, if you didn't know the word for Turkish bath, you would not understand the gold embossed letters above the doors that welcome you to the sixteenth-century Çemberlıtaş Hamam.[15]

I have been visiting this hamam for decades, joining the centuries of women who have made the same pilgrimage. Historically, the Turkish hamam evolved from the Roman bath, a civilized public space that showcased the engineering feat of piping, heating, and cooling water in cities. Traditionally, locals gathered on gender-specific days in their village hamam to exchange gossip, escape domestic duties, arrange marriages, and celebrate bridal parties. These days, women still linger in the hamam. So do I.

---

15 A hamam is a traditional Turkish bathhouse featuring a marble steam room, scrubbing services, and massages, separated by gender.

In past visits to Turkey, I have taken my daughters to the hamam, but they haven't lived the feminine journey long enough to appreciate its powerful effect. Of course, on *Lost Women of Turkey Pilgrimages*, I bring the women here, whose fresh encounter gives me more words for the restorative and transformative experience that exists in this utterly foreign place.

From the moment we enter the hamam, an otherworldly atmosphere engulfs us. Ancient Ottoman script hangs above the entrance where we receive our very thin and very small towel and disposable undergarment. An attendant leads us to a changing cabin and waits for us to emerge with these provisions. She escorts us through a lounge, lined on one side by a low divan and capped by a station serving fresh orange juice or Turkish coffee, and then pushes open a thick wooden door into a wall of steam. The interior of the bath is entirely white marble. Light shines down from the domed ceiling above through small, recessed circles onto an enormous, heated marble slab in the middle of the room. Encircling the slab are four arched doorways that lead to little rooms. Each room is rimmed with a low step and features three marble fountains with both hot and cold brass water faucets, as well as a copper bowl floating in the basin.

We gather on the step, awkwardly arranging our "towels" around our naked bodies, anxious in all the ways, and begin to douse ourselves with water: hot, cold, lukewarm, cold, cold, cold. It is hot and we are sweaty. I have tried to describe this experience to the women with me, to prepare them, but it is useless. We are basically strangers to one another at this point in the trip, and our vulnerability, our bodies' stories, all of it, is raging inside as the first of the "hamam ladies" comes into our alcove. Naked, save the little panties barely visible beneath her tummy, she reaches for the first woman, pulls her to her feet, rips the towel off as she arranges it on the slab, and gestures to lie atop. As more "hamam ladies" come for the women of our group, the marble slab fills with our naked bodies, and the scrubbing commences. Then the singing, as the ladies hum and sing and scrub, their bare flesh hanging over ours.

And the strangest thing begins to happen.

Their gruff, indelicate washing, non-sensual as it is, allows for a shift in those whose body has often felt objectified. The way they slap our butt cheeks to flip us over and then pull us up to scrub our hair feels oddly nurturing to those who long to be mothered, still. And the way their bare bellies and breasts slap against our skin normalizes our own flesh that we have covered with so much shame through the years.

As we return to the fountains in the alcove, we marvel at our smooth skin, and something else. Something sacred. Just beginning to put words to the feeling, it will continue to work itself out the rest of the week. As we get to know one another better, leaving the ancient Ottoman city of Istanbul to continue our pilgrimage, we will repeatedly express how surprised we were, how nourished we felt in the hamam. It will be the highlight of the trip, the most considerable risk yielding the greatest gift. And slowly, we will wonder if we left our body shame behind that thick wooden door. Is this what women have known for hundreds of years—a mystery we have only just discovered? Is it possible? Could the steam of this ancient hamam evaporate shame? At the very least, the question is one of the treasures we bring home from this exotic land. And it's why I'll return.[16]

---

16 Adapted from author's original post "Shame Walks into Steam," *Red Tent Living*, October 2022.

❧

I've read that the hamam was the soul of Syria, central to the social fabric of Egypt, and was so popular in Victorian England that the Titanic included one. The Ottomans may not have invented the bathhouse, but they certainly loved and proliferated hamams; it is thought that at the height of the empire, there were 2,500. Sultans' wives built many. The small entrance fees were used to fund neighborhood foundations that included a mosque, a school, a soup kitchen, a hospital, and more. For example, Cemberlitaş Hamam was built by Nurbanu Sultan to support her foundation in Üsküdar, on the other side of the Bosphorus Strait. For this reason, for hundreds of years, hamams were not privately owned. They were symbols of sultanic rule, meant to convey care for the public and justify the sultanate.

Hamams did indeed arise out of a value for cleanliness, but were not merely used for purification, like the Jewish Mikvah. They were certainly functional, declining in use after plumbing became a standard feature in new home constructions, but they were so much more. I often try to liken it to something relatable in the modern West, especially for women. A book club? A play group? A yoga class?

Imagine the only space free of men where women gathered leisurely. They packed their lunch alongside soap, towels, and slippers, and brought along their young children to spend the day at the neighborhood hamam. Moving in and out of the cold and hot rooms, they gossiped, evaluated potential daughters-in-law, and strutted their wealth. Their slippers were far from the plastic slip-ons provided in today's Turkish baths. They were bejeweled showcases of class. And if you were poor, you were barefoot. I have several old copper soap containers with slats in the bottom, used to carry homemade soap to and from the hamam. Did the larger one indicate wealth, more children, or nothing at all? I don't know. So much is still unknown.

When the Ottoman Empire crumbled during World War I and Mustafa Kemal Atatürk led the new Turkish Republic in its modernization and Europeanization, an intentional distancing from the past occurred. Even the use of the word "Ottoman" was replaced by "forefathers." Hagia Sophia (the great sixth-century Byzantine church) was converted from a mosque to a museum in a matter of months to highlight its ancient heritage rather than the more recent Ottoman and Islamic one. Atatürk wanted a secular society.

And so, gradually over the last century, the hamam faded into the background. While completing research on the specific hamam I keep returning to, it was found that Turks fall into five categories: Some have never been and refuse to go to the hamam, claiming they are unhygienic; some have never been, but are embarrassed by this, feeling that tourists know more about their history than they do; another group has been a few times as internal tourists; still another group would like to go, but haven't found a reason to yet; and the last group embraces tradition and regularly goes out of enjoyment.[17] This final group still organizes bridal parties and henna nights, forty days post-birth mom and baby rituals, or the after-circumcision party.[18]

---

17 Nina Cichocki, "Continuity and Change in Turkish Bathing Culture in Istanbul: The Life Story of the Çemberlitaş Hamam," *Turkish Studies* 6, no. 1 (March 2005): 93–112, https://doi.org/10.10 80/1468384042000339348.

18 It's an ancient custom in the entire Middle East for new moms

They crave history and tradition, longing to be rooted in something bigger and anchored in a glorious past.

The last group describes the afternoon my daughter and I spent at the hamam, where a group of young Turkish women entered, singing, laughing, and celebrating a bride-to-be. It explains the local membership program that the hamam offers to incentivize and normalize usage by locals. It also explains the recently renovated Zeyrek Çinili Hamam, a thirteen-year-long project by the Marmara Group on a 500-year-old hamam, located far from the regular tourist path. It seems that alongside myself, there is an increased interest in the history of this city, particularly among Istanbulites.

Personally, I am drawn to spaces that safely bring women together. In all that I've read about the hamam, including how it is often a place for class distinction, the spread of news and political conspiracies, and matchmaking, I have yet to read about body comparison being an issue. It's interesting that the thing I believe women struggle with most in our American culture seemed absent in theirs—as if the hamam ritual created a normalization of body diversity. If the hamam has anything to do with erasing body shame, then I want more.

After our first pilgrimage to Turkey, with my sixteen-year-old daughter in tow, she and I lingered a few days to catch our breath. Our pilgrimage concludes at a lovely hotel on the Aegean Sea, equipped with its own Starbucks and hamam. I will return to this hotel for as long as I am able because I contend

---

to wait forty days before leaving the home with their newborn. This tradition has both superstitious and health roots.

it is a slice of heaven on earth. My daughter wanted to board a ferry and add another country to our list; the Greek island of Samos was only an hour away. I wanted to reserve a cabana, get a massage, and explore every room in the spa: the rainfall room, the salt room, the steam room, the snow room. The stress I had carried from leading the first pilgrimage could now ease, and I needed to unwind.

Furthermore, we had one computer with us, and I wanted to linger at Starbucks, overlooking the sea, and write; she wanted to start editing the interviews she had conducted throughout our journey. In the end, we compromised. We both got everything we wanted, but it was truncated.

On our designated spa day, we tentatively entered the changing room and the corridor beyond, being newbies to spas in general and Turkish five-star ones in particular. We lay side by side in the singular lounge chair in the blue-tinted salt room until we admitted our doubt that anything was actually happening. We pushed the wrong button in the steam room, and an attendant showed up with that all-too-familiar "tsk, tsk" shaming. We dumped buckets of water on ourselves in the rainfall room, warmed to breathlessness in the sauna, and gave up on the seemingly broken snow room. Having exhausted all of the little rooms on that side of the hallway, we ventured toward a dimly lit pool and the large wooden door at the end of the corridor. We were all alone and therefore far more brazen than we would typically have been. Was it me or Sophie who opened it? I cannot remember, but we entered to discover our very own hamam.

As is common in resort hotels, this Turkish bath was co-ed and a replica of the ancient designs. The same marble circular slab filled the middle of the room. The ceiling was domed, with small circles cut out to let in light, and six tiled alcoves encircled the room, each with a marble basin and two copper faucets. I had a quick flash of holding a naked baby against my body in a similar hotel hamam and remembered Sophie, fifteen years before. Modern hotel hamams are pristine. The white marble glistens, the vibrant blues and reds of the Iznik tiles unfaded. Unlike the sixteenth-century Cemberlitaş Hamam in Istanbul, there are no cracks or peeling paint on the walls. We turned on the hot and cold faucets of one basin and doused ourselves with water using the small copper bowl set inside.

After we were thoroughly soaked, I invited Sophie to lie down on the marble slab, and I began pouring hot water over her, from feet to head, and then from head to feet, over and over. I cannot hold her little body against mine anymore, but this was as tender a moment as we'd shared in a long time. Her eyes stayed closed, an invitation to continue, and I poured bowl upon bowl upon bowl. It had been such a gift to travel with her, to see her come alive to new foods, accents, and challenges, and to watch her try to capture it all with her camera. I knew I'd awakened something that would lead to her departure—gave her confidence in herself and the world that would yield an adventurer. I can't help expanding her dreams, always casting a vision for something even bigger than she imagined, even though I know what I'm inevitably creating. I tossed water on her torso, and I knew: I was raising a young adult who was already halfway gone. Her presence on the trip, younger by ten years than the youngest participant, had been stunning. She slid right into deep conversations, offered words of blessing one woman needed, and was aware of and generously allowed another to feel mothered as she watched our relationship. She had been a companion more than a teenage daughter. And yet there, in the bath, she craved my nurture. We all long to be mothered.

Eventually, a Filipino woman came to fetch us to begin the massage process, leading us to another room where she instructed us to lie with cucumbers on our eyes. From there, we ended up on side-by-side tables, face down and eyes wide, when the women straddled our backs and began kneading our muscles with their elbows. Needless to say, the spa experience did not exactly conclude in a relaxing manner.

When I return to the hamam with the third pilgrimage, the "hamam ladies" come into the chamber bare-breasted and then, surprisingly, put on bikini tops. Perhaps tourists have complained? Maybe it's related to hygiene? My lady is so short that we are eye to eye as I sit on the marble slab and she scrubs one arm, then another. Her belly is so firm, so round, it nearly touches mine. She smiles and softly hums. It sounds outrageous as I think it, but as I lie down, I miss the breasts hanging and flopping over me in such an unprecious way that it approximates nurture. Later, when I am clothed and seek her out with a tip, she emerges from a room bare-breasted again. I catch myself before I laugh at the inconsistency.

Because every year brings something different into focus for me during the pilgrimage, this year I am keenly aware of the round room around me, the dome ceiling, the water flowing, and the steam filling. We are in a womb! And the nourishment we receive feels akin to what we surely received in our own mothers' wombs. I imagine the women of the harem: girls in their twenties, already mothers and required to mother the newly arrived adolescents freshly stolen from their own mothers.

How did those new girls hold the ambivalence of both craving and repelling the care offered to them as they adjusted to older concubines bathing them, preparing them for the sultan? How do I hold my own ambivalence about receiving care from the "hamam ladies"?

The year I notice the womb-like room, my search for the mothering of God will guide my eyes to new treasures in the Turkish landscape. Thomas Merton's words will serve as a faithful reminder: *The geographical pilgrimage is the symbolic acting out of an inner journey.* It's a year of my own maternal transition, and I'm in need of nurture. Although many steps will be the same, I'll see familiar places differently and experience God uniquely. Many times I'll feel as brave as I did the first time I entered the hamam, but even more, I'll feel small, tender, and in desperate need of mothering.

> *How would it feel to be in a space like the hamam? Which piece of the hamam resonated with you—nurturing, body shame, mothering, or something else? What does that piece tell you about your younger self, your current self, or your desired future self?*

ÇAY

Typically enjoyed in the cold room after bathing in the hot room, Turkish tea gained popularity when coffee was scarce during World War I. It is now consumed far more than coffee, with Turks having five or more glasses at all times of the day. Pouring tea for guests is the quintessential sign of Turkish hospitality. In Turkey, tea is prepared with a double teapot, using tea grown in the Black Sea region, and served in small tulip-shaped glasses accompanied by sugar cubes on a saucer. To make this without Turkish tea (although you can easily buy Turkish tea online), substitute with black tea. Alternatively, Turks love apple tea, which, on the plus side, is decaffeinated!

KAHVE

I have secured passes for each of us that are preloaded with the number of swipes we'll need on public transport. The joy I have in this small convenience is another private knowing I tuck away. There is no way for the women to comprehend what a day in my life was like in 1997, when we first moved to Istanbul to work with students, yet every turn is laden with memories for me. During our time on this pilgrimage, we will be using only ferries, trams, funiculars, and trolleys (aside from airport transfers and flights, of course), and they will all accept this magical little card as payment.

My husband and I arrived in Istanbul all those years ago to join a newly formed campus ministry team led by Turks. The directors were recently appointed Turks, and they lived in a suburban, affordable area of the endlessly sprawling mega-city (far from college campuses). The previous team of Americans had set up apartments near these leaders, and so, after two days of basic orientation in a two-star hotel on the European side of the city, we piled into a couple of taxis with our bags and fellow teammates and drove to our new homes on the Asian side.[19]

Our building was a plain, green, six-story block, and our unit was on the fourth floor. The other new American couple helped

---

19 Istanbul is divided by the Bosphorus Strait into the European and Asian side. It's the only city in the world that spans two continents.

us with our bags, and we crammed into the elevator, unable to read the warning written in Turkish that no more than two people should use it at a time. We made it as far as the middle of the first and second floors before coming to a complete stop, where we remained trapped until someone found the building manager, who then found someone to pry open the doors for us to climb out. It wasn't a great start to our relationship with that manager. When we finally entered the small apartment and saw the lime green couch with purple accents and the cardboard box serving as a "table" with two white plastic chairs, I held my tears until our teammates left to find their apartment building, bursting into sobs as soon as we were alone. The city already felt unbearable.

A few days later, the four of us started the daily trek to language school. Our teammates walked ten minutes up the hill toward us because our flat was closest to the highway bus stops, where each bus had a driver and a man in a booth behind him collecting money. We stood on the crowded bus for thirty minutes as it traversed neighborhoods to the main road toward the Kadıköy ferry terminal. We exited at the bus terminal and speed-walked to catch our twenty-five-minute ferry to Eminönü, as missing it would mean taking the ferry to Karaköy instead and walking across the Galata Bridge and Golden Horn. From Eminönü, we could get the tram up to Beyazıt Square near the grand entrance to Istanbul University; however, there was rarely room to squeeze into the tram. So, we usually walked up the cobblestone streets behind the Egyptian Spice Bazaar all the way to Beyazıt, around to the other side of the fifteenth-century gated campus entrance to walk down a street we would come to christen "Little Calcutta."

The street felt like another vestige of history left behind in the modernization of this urban landscape. Small openings in stone walls revealed blacksmiths, coal deposits, and our favorite, an oven with a baker who was always just pulling out fresh bread scooped up by young boys sent to restock market bins or fulfill restaurant orders. The smell overpowered the coal for just a few feet, and we hungrily bought our loaf to eat on the rest of the walk to the Istanbul University Language Department. Here, we joined international students hoping to pass the proficiency test to begin their studies at this prestigious, ancient university. We sat with Jordanians, Somalians, Eritreans, and Russians. As the only Americans in class, we never revealed our sole purpose in learning Turkish was to share our faith, not to enroll in degree programs.

Though we were at Istanbul University, most students there did not speak English, which meant to do student ministry, we needed to travel to other English-speaking campuses. And so, after a morning of class, we walked back down the hill to the Golden Horn and got a bus along the Bosphorus, where we transferred at Beşiktaş to get on another bus inland. By the time we arrived at the smoke-filled canteens, students were nearing the end of their day and eager to start their long journeys home (most lived with family somewhere in the city), as were we. The futility of these days was immensely discouraging.

We took seven boats and buses each day until we added campuses only reachable by mini-bus, shared taxis, or private boats, where the fare was passed up to the driver and change was passed back to the passenger. This was also a time before the Akbil—a reloadable button—existed, which could be used on city transport, and before the subway was completed beneath the Bosphorus. We dealt in coins and crowds and the daily crisscrossing of continents.

We learned where to enter the ferry to get the best spot outside, away from smokers. We learned that when you say "Inecek Var," the minibus stops and opens its doors. We discovered that there was a Mexican restaurant in Levent and a very Western-looking café in Maslak. We lived on quick and easy street food— fresh bread for breakfast, grilled cheese for lunch, and pizza for dinner—yet we lost weight from all the walking.

The city was eating us alive, and yet we were also thriving paradoxically. One word quickly turned into entire conversations in Turkish. We negotiated for new furniture and its delivery ourselves, replacing the lime couch with a used blue set that would reappear in intern apartments for the next ten years. We sat on the deck of boats at night as we crossed the magical Bosphorus to return home, watching the lights atop the Hagia Sophia minarets change colors according to the holiday. And then, a couple of students placed their faith in Jesus, and all seemed so rewarding. One year turned into ten.

There was nothing quite like that first year—before kids, before we had a car. The chaotic concrete sprawl became so familiar, even now, twenty-five years later, I know exactly where we are going and the various options to get us there. I'm just so delighted to have one preloaded payment card that will get us on every one of those options.

My husband and I debated whether we should buy a car in Istanbul. After that first year, we came back to live long-term. By then, we had a one-year-old and were set to become the city campus leaders for our organization. We'd be the only family and the only permanent staff. Wouldn't it be nice to drive everyone to retreats or the shopping center? Wouldn't it be nice for me to go places with a toddler without taking the bus or a taxi? We didn't know how to do this sort of thing in another country, but we had heard other foreigners talk about a car auction outside of the city. And that's where we found the "Dragon Wagon"—a black VW ten-passenger van used mainly by professional transport companies. This is what we thought we needed. The Dragon Wagon would become my "soccer mom" van in the mega-city of Istanbul!

At the time, we lived in Moda, a tiny neighborhood on a hill atop the huge transit district of Kadıköy: ancient Chalcedon and "city of the blind," where the Council of Chalcedon took place in 451 CE. When we lived there, it was a "district" of Istanbul through which 2.5 million people passed every day. There were four city ferry ports, a dozen private boat lines, a bus terminal, a mini-bus terminal, a shared taxi terminal, and a historic trolley. The trolley came up to Moda before turning to go back down the central shopping vein of Kadıköy. There was only one, one-way road in and out of Moda. That's how narrow most streets were, and where they were wider, cars parked every which way on either side.

We bought the van in a moment of insanity. My husband told me to forget everything I knew about driving defensively. I would need to learn how to drive offensively to survive this city. We put the car seat in the back, all by itself among the other seven seats, and most days it was just my toddler and me navigating the crazy streets of Moda. I made it out of our parking area, along the one-way route past "stinky canal," past Fenerbahçe stadium, and to the nearest shopping center with a parking garage and a Carrefour where my son could drive a car attached to a grocery cart, and I could shop without talking to anyone. On the days when a vehicle randomly blocked the tiny alleys or my designated parking spot on our lane, I learned to leave the keys in the ignition, get out, and look like a helpless foreign woman. Within no time, a man would jump into my driver's seat and get the van out of whatever pickle it was in. Always with a head shake and tsk tsk, but I was more than happy to sacrifice my pride to male chauvinism for the assistance.

⊰

One day, as my two-year-old and I were leaving Kiddieland on the top floor of that shopping center, I noticed a very familiar logo. It is no exaggeration to say that I nearly collapsed right there in the middle of the mall. There, on the floor below, across the atrium, a huge "Coming Soon" sign promised that in the near future, Starbucks would be coming to Turkey. We stalked that sign for months with no visible change, until my husband finally crawled beneath a gap in the gate to ask for a date: "Spring." We waited and waited for specifics, and finally it was announced: March 2003. Our entire team joined us on the opening day of the first location, celebrating the arrival of what would become a sight more common than any other Western chain. Despite the exorbitant price of the coffee compared to the Turkish options next door, young Turks couldn't get enough of the famous medusa, and locations soon sprang up all over the country. As of 2025, there were about 700 Starbucks in Turkey.

One month after Starbucks opened, I went into labor on the day of our neighborhood street bazaar. The one way out of the neighborhood was straight through the middle of the bazaar, which at the time was the largest in the nation, and we must have been quite the sight as we honked our way through the crowd. Ella came fast and furious and was with us within half an hour of our arrival at the ER. The hospital was affiliated with Harvard, and my doctor spoke English, but the experience of giving birth in Turkey was still utterly foreign. The newly opened Starbucks down the street offered a small taste of comfort the next morning when my husband brought me a scone and a decaf latte for breakfast.

Starbucks became a little space of retreat for us expats. In those early days, the first branch was full of foreigners, as it was the only cafe that didn't allow smoking and served filtered coffee, not Nescafé. And the irony is not lost on me. In the land where coffee proliferated, our betrayal was great, but spoke to the degree of our cultural fatigue.

Coffee was first imported into Istanbul from Yemen by Süleyman the Magnificent and became an integral part of palace culture. A new position was created, Chief Coffee Maker, and these appointees were so trusted that they often later became Grand Viziers.[20] By 1554, the first public coffeehouse opened, and soon after, there were supposedly fifty-five coffee houses around Tahmis Sokak (the Roasted and Ground Coffee Street) by the Golden Horn port. The Egyptian Spice Bazaar (completed in 1663) opens onto Tahmis Sokak and it remains the largest spice market in the world. Coffee was a major export, and it was through this port that it proliferated through Europe.

I wonder if the female sultans who built the Egyptian Spice

---

20 A Grand Vizier was akin to the combined Chief of Staff and Chairman of the Joint Chief of Staffs to the sultan. During the Sultanate of Woman, he rivaled the Valide Sultan in influence. If they were allies, the empire flourished. If enemies, their rivalry could end in death.

Bazaar and the surrounding mosque complex (food kitchen, school, bathhouse, and more), which the market funded, knew that coffeehouses would be where political dissention was sown, where plotting occurred. Were they favorable to the Janissaries, keeping their powerful husbands, sons, and competitors in check? Coffeehouses quickly became the male social gathering places in lieu of bars (an empire that didn't drink alcohol!) and were deemed a considerable threat to sultans. Remember, in 1622, at age eighteen, Osman Sultan was strangled, supposedly by his Janissaries, because he ordered the coffeehouses to be shut down. As a result, his brother, Murad IV, grew up in fear of a Janissary revolt—and the meeting places that could encourage one.

By 1633, coffeehouses were seen as the seedbed of revolution. Imagine a place accessible to all classes. A space that required lingering, for it took twenty minutes to brew Turkish coffee and then another ten for the hot, steaming elixir to cool enough to sip, and then at least ten more to drink due to its bitterness and thickness. In that space, entire insurrections could be schemed. Murad IV passed a law ordering the decapitation of anyone seen drinking coffee, and was known to be the most brutal of all Ottoman rulers if caught in violation. He didn't close down the export of coffee, nor did he go after the practice outside of Istanbul, but if you were caught enjoying a cup in the capital, off with your head!

As with anything forbidden, coffee drinking flourished amidst this prohibition. In the same way Starbucks would multiply in the early twenty-first century, the Ottoman coffeehouse rapidly spread in the seventeenth century. Until 1871, raw beans were roasted and ground at home, but when Mehmet Efendi decided to roast and grind beans right at the corner of Tahmis

Sokak, which sat at the entrance to the Egyptian Spice Bazaar, everything changed again. And that little shop, 150 years later, is still there, still selling coffee grounds, still sending its aromas wafting into the crowded streets.

✍

At the end of our first day, I lead the women from Leyla's Turkish Delight shop, through the bustling streets to the Egyptian Spice Bazaar, down the side alley to Tahmis Sokak, past Mehmet Efendi's coffee roaster, and into a restored inn for our own cup of Turkish coffee. We have nearly made it through Day One. All in all, we have traveled more on foot than on public transportation, and this boost of caffeine will help us with the final trek up the hill to our boutique inn for the evening. Tonight, as we gather around the table, we will recount the ways our senses have been on alert today, the many ways the harem lingers in our souls, and the general overwhelm that can't be helped after our first day in this city.

The waiter brings our Turkish coffee with a small square of rose lokum on the saucer, and after sipping the sweet, thick elixir, I explain some past times shared in the salons of Turkish women.[21] From its beginning, coffee was never *just* a drink. From conspiracy to fortune telling, the little cup has always been the center of culture.[22] In fact, UNESCO added Turkish

---

21 A "salon" is the open concept, living-dining room of a Turkish home.

22 And actually, there was far more than *just* a little cup! In the palace and wealthy homes, the entire coffee service could take up to seven people holding various elements and serving various roles to achieve the whole experience.

coffee culture and tradition to the Representative List of the Intangible Cultural Heritage of Humanity in 2013. One of Turkey's wedding traditions involves brides preparing coffee for potential grooms. If she liked a suitor, she put sugar in the cup. Supposedly, for fun and spice, these days, during the same ritual, a bride will put salt in her groom's cup to test his patience. Women will also turn the cup over and read the grounds left behind, telling the fortune of their friend. There are even multiple apps that will analyze the prophetic message in your grounds. I turn mine upside down on the saucer and peek inside. All I see are muddy lines.

As women, it has been a difficult day of difficult stories. The feminine history of the Ottoman Empire has been confusing as we confront the inescapable duality of power and enslavement in the harem; the co-mingling of shame and nurture, freedom and attunement in the hamam; and the heightened sense of genderism in this complicated part of a complicated city in a complicated country. *İşte Turkey*. This is Turkey. Day One. Welcome.

As you consider the themes we explored in Ottoman Istanbul, what resonates with you? The duality of influence and erasure in the harem? The co-mingling of shame and nurture in the hamam? The complexity of honor and power symbolically tasted in the sweet and salty Turkish Delight? And if you were to read your coffee grounds, what might you see?

KAHVE

You'll need small demitasse or espresso cups, ideally a cezve (a small pot with a long handle that can be placed directly on the stove), as well as dark coffee grounds the consistency of flour (you may need to use an industrial grinder) to make Turkish coffee.

1. Add 1 ½ demitasse cups of cold water (approximately 3 ounces or 90 ml), 1 tablespoon of coffee grounds, and ½ to 2 teaspoons of sugar (based on your sweet preference) to the cezve. If you prefer it even creamier, use milk instead of water and/or add a bit of milk to the cezve.
2. Stir once and do not stir again!
3. Heat on the stovetop until it starts to foam and rise. Remove from the heat and skim off the foam into the cups. Then, return the mixture to the stove and repeat the process (approximately 10 minutes total).
4. Pour into the demitasse cups and do not add anything to it at this point, unless you want to sprinkle ground cardamom or pistachios on top (espresso cups work as well).

PART 2

CONSTANTINOPLE: INSCRIBING ON COLUMNS

4TH-9TH CENTURIES

ON DAY TWO of our pilgrimage, we travel backward in time, changing empires from Ottoman Istanbul to Byzantine Constantinople—the same streets, the same stones, the same buildings.[23] Every turn in the old city engulfs us in layers of history and the fingerprints of women who have shaped it. Constantinople was a city of legends, Byzantium an empire of mystery. Lasting longer than the Roman Empire, we owe far more to Byzantium for our faith, art, and knowledge, yet know far less about it than Rome. One thousand years before Hürrem fell in love with Süleyman, Theodora fell in love with Justinian. The impact of those seemingly loving, mutually respectful marriages is still felt throughout Istanbul and beyond.

As we exit our little hotel, we walk beneath the remains of the Byzantine Boukolean Palace, belonging to Emperor Justinian and Empress Theodora. Yet around the corner, Ottoman-era

---

23 When Constantine became sole emperor of Rome and made the new capital Constantinople in 324 CE, the Byzantine Empire began and lasted until Mehmed conquered it in 1453. For the purposes of the pilgrimage, we focus on the fourth through ninth centuries.

wood houses share walls with Starbucks and Burger King. The craziness of this part of the city makes my familiarity and comfort in it all the more wild. I never lose the sensation of how at ease I am in this brand of chaos. This was the place I became an adult and suffered some of my greatest tragedies. Every step I take is palatable with the younger version of a Beth I am proud of and also want to squeeze (and sometimes slap). We are every age we've ever been.[24] Often, we need to go and be a stranger to remember those ages. On the trail of Byzantine women, we are given clues to find ourselves.

The irony of our journey backward in time is that as we go back, we discover that women held more visible influence and were less obscure. It's the opposite of what we all assume, but when we look for their stories, we find women exerted power and led in surprising ways, especially within the church. And for our pilgrimage, another day in Istanbul strips a little more away of our own obscurity.

---

24 This saying is generally attributed to Madeleine L'Engle.

MONOGRAMS

I LEAD THE women down the street from our Istanbul hotel, away from the hustle and bustle of the tourist area. Just one block over sits a red brick mosque called Little Hagia Sophia, a deceiving name since this small ancient mosque-church is nothing like her big, grand sister (Hagia Sophia) up the hill. We enter the courtyard and step to the side, covering our heads with scarves, so I can tell them the story. It's a good story.

And it's a story I've only recently learned about, as this is another building I never visited in all the years I lived here. From the outset, it appears to be a typical Byzantine church converted into a mosque.[25] One minaret shoots to the sky from behind the octagonal domed roof, and from our vantage point, the remains of ancient walls line the opposite side of the courtyard.[26] It is Day Two, and the women are already saturated with walls like these;

---

25 When the Ottomans took over the city, they converted nearly every church into a mosque.

26 A minaret is a tall, slim tower connected to a mosque from which the Call to Prayer is given. The larger the role the mosque plays in a neighborhood, the more minarets it has.

we pass by various stages of ruin and reconstruction everywhere we turn in this part of the old city.

But the walls we pause near are not city walls. No, these particular stones make up the walls of an old palace connected to this church, the original Church of Saints Sergius and Bacchus, dedicated to two fourth-century martyrs whom Justinian claimed spared him a traitor's death in the early sixth century. And so, the Emperor Justinian and his wife, Empress Theodora, had this church built as an annex to the palace in which they resided. Though the palace is long gone, the church remains. Well, the mosque it became in the 1500s remains, hence the head coverings.

The story I tell the women in the courtyard is one of intrigue and deceit, theological nuance and politicking. It's challenging for our modern Western minds to grasp the gravity of the situation that led our heroine to do the things I'm about to describe. It requires a deep dive into early church history, the various church councils, and some context regarding the Christian climate of the time. I try to explain micro- and macro-narratives: the choices women make as a composite of both their own story and the culture and historical context of their time.

As a quick summary, I explain that the first Christ-followers were a sect of Judaism, causing significant disruption to the Roman-Jewish equilibrium as internal debate created more unrest (remember who demanded Jesus' crucifixion). This led to Roman *and* Jewish persecution of Christians, on and off, for most of the second and third centuries. During this time, and despite the threat of death, the church grew and developed an informal leadership structure that included bishops, deacons, and deaconesses. And then Constantine became the sole emperor of the Roman Empire in 324 CE. He converted to

Christianity, but more importantly, under his rule, a fusion of politics and religion began in the new capital, Constantinople.

Constantine inherited a fractured, ununified Christianity. At the time, the primary debate among church leaders centered on the Trinity. To bring stability to the empire, he called for a church council, the first of its kind, to be held in a little town outside of what is today the megapolis of Istanbul, but then must have been a day's journey from Constantinople: Iznik. You know it as Nicea. The Council of Nicea was not so well attended for 325 CE (of ~1800 bishops, only ~318 attended), and the creed that came from it, while we know it as orthodox today, did not quell all of the debate. In fact, six more church councils were held over the next few hundred years, continuing to argue the nuance of the essence of Jesus.

Which brings us to the courtyard of the Little Hagia Sophia.

The year my youngest returned to Turkey for the first time since leaving at age one, she was in sixth-grade world history with a marvelous teacher. When they came to the unit on empires, she excitedly came home each day with fun new facts about ancient Constantinople. Having played virtual tour guide to hundreds of visitors, I nodded knowingly as she talked about Constantine the Great, Emperor Justinian, the Nika Riots, and the Hagia Sophia, her namesake. And then one day she came home talking about the Empress Theodora—Justinian's wife. I stopped nodding.

In all my years of living in that city, telling tourists about her history, and taking them to the church Theodora apparently built, I never *knew* about her. My daughter's little name drop sent me diving into Theodora's life, learning that she championed women's rights, child protection laws, and general human rights legislation. I became so enamored with her that I told Sophie we would be going to the Hagia Sophia that summer and not leaving until we found evidence of Theodora. How had I missed the entire legacy of such an amazing woman?

When the day finally arrived, we entered the museum and headed straight for the upper-level mosaics, which depicted Byzantine emperors and empresses. I assumed Theodora was in one of these mosaics and I hadn't realized it before. As we lingered before each one, matching the Greek letters in the mosaic to the placard on the wall, we struck out. After covering every square inch of the massive building, our legs were throbbing, and we sat down on some chairs tucked into an alcove in front of a small TV screen. A documentary was playing in English, but we weren't really paying attention until we heard her name. *Theodora.*

As I looked at the screen, I saw the camera zoom in on one of the column capitals. I had noticed an unusual design on each, but hadn't realized the designs entailed four different Greek monograms: Justinian, Emperor, Empress, and Theodora. Sophie and I looked at each other and wordlessly jumped up to return to the nave of the church to find her. Tears brimmed as I stared up at the evidence. Her fingerprints, her actual name, were here on this building, and as I would later discover, all of the ones she commissioned. I was breathless.

Finding Theodora changed the way I see the world. She changed how I travel, looking for the stories of the women who helped shape the cities I explore. She changed how I understand history, reading in between the lines and making meaning from what is not recorded. And she changed how I accept my own humanity, as she became a guide to embracing my complex glory.

∽

Theodora was born in the late fifth century CE. Her father was a bear keeper, and her mother and sister were performers in the hippodrome, the Roman amphitheater. Eventually, she too became an actor, and in those days, that profession was synonymous with prostitution. One of her wealthy patrons made Theodora his mistress and took her with him when he returned to North Africa. Her time there is unclear, but it is believed that she had a child and met Bishop Timothy of Alexandria, where she became not only a Christian, but a devoted Miaphysite (one who believes that Christ was fully human and fully divine in one unified nature).

It is unclear why she and her child returned to Constantinople, but soon after she met and fell in love with Justinian, heir to the throne of the Byzantine Empire. They waited for his uncle to change the laws, allowing him to marry a former actor, and soon after they wed, they became Emperor and Empress. The acts attributed to Theodora are great: She abolished sex slavery, opened a home for former prostitutes called Metanoia (which means repentance), increased legal rights for divorced women, including property and child custody, instituted the death penalty for rape, and removed the death penalty for women caught in adultery. In fact, her name appeared in every law passed during their reign, and new legislation ceased the year she died.

Despite all that they accomplished together for the empire, Justinian and Theodora were on opposite sides of the Christian-political spectrum. She was a Miaphysite, while Justinian followed the decision made at the Council of Chalcedon (held in 451 CE) that Jesus was both fully human and fully divine, in two distinct natures. In the conflation of church and state, bishops were deposed and exiled periodically, depending on the politicization of the capital. And even the two rival chariot teams, the Blues and Greens, represented not just two different political factions, but the ecumenical council they aligned with.

In 532 CE, Justinian had been on a building spree and had significantly increased taxes to fund it. His spending already made him unpopular, yet when a disturbance broke out during a chariot race in the hippodrome, he incited the people even more by arresting and giving the death sentence to one of the famous racers. At the next race, leaders of both the Blues and the Greens petitioned the emperor for mercy, and when he refused, riots erupted. The Nika Riots killed some thirty thousand and burned most of the city to the ground, including the Hagia Sophia Church. Justinian prepared to abandon the city when Theodora famously told him: "Whether or not a woman should give an example of courage to men is neither here nor there… I think that flight, even if it brings us to safety, is not in our interest. Every man born to see the light of day must die. But that one who has been emperor should become an exile, I cannot bear."[27] She convinced him to stay and rebuild.

I bring the women to the little mosque-church annexed to the old palace because it's the best illustration of Theodora's

---

27 Procopius was a contemporary historian who painted Theodora in a very negative light. He claims the death toll was 35,000. Procopius, *History of the Wars* 1.24.33–38 (Theodora's address to Justinian and the council, January 532). Standard English: H. B. Dewing, Loeb Classical Library 48 (Cambridge, MA: Harvard University Press, 1914). Online text with section numbers: LacusCurtius (U. Chicago).

badassery. Her monogram is here, too, along with an inscription about her: "God Crown; she whose piety enlightens the soul; whose ceaseless activity and unremitting good works bring relief to those who are crushed by poverty." But what is no longer visible is the secret passageway that led to the palace, the means by which she hid eight bishops for twelve years.

Remember, she was not an adherent to the Council of Chalcedon's decision that Jesus had two distinct natures. As a Miaphysite, she used her power to bring fellow Miaphysite sympathizer, Bishop Anthimus, to Constantinople as Patriarch.[28] When the Pope found out about this move, he had him deposed, and Theodora hid Anthimus, along with other bishops, in the palace. What does this tell us about her actual role in the church? Was this an example of the conflation of power and religion? Or was this another clue to how she was viewed and the power she held, just like the Ravenna mosaic is a clue?[29] It begs the question: How did people really view her? Or, perhaps more poignantly, what roles did she actually hold?

Theodora's persistent protection of persecuted Miaphysites may have had far more historical consequences than she ever imagined or wanted. The debate between Chalcedonians and Miaphysites over Jesus' nature was divisive, and the bishops of the Eastern church (Coptic, Syrian, Armenian) were

---

28 Every church had a bishop, as they served as overseers or pastors. There were five large cities with a patriarch, all equal. The pope was the patriarch of Rome, revered by the Eastern church as most honorable, but not most powerful.

29 In the San Vitale Basilica in Ravenna (c. 547 CE), Theodora is pictured wearing a purple robe symbolic of a military and imperial ruler, and she is holding the eucharist, something only the bishop and the emperor, as God's divine representative, would do.

exiled, excommunicated, and even killed because they were Miaphysites. The division weakened the relatively young church to such a degree that many in the East abandoned the faith altogether. Theodora had no way of knowing that fifty years after her death, a prophet would rise to popularity in Arabia and, relatively easily, convert most of the peninsula and former Eastern Orthodox lands to Islam in less than 100 years.

Tradition tells us that on her deathbed, she made Justinian promise to protect her beloved Miaphysite monks and bishops in Egypt, many of whom were hiding in the Sinai desert. The year she died, Justinian began construction on what is now known as St. Catherine's Monastery. In the middle of the Sinai Peninsula, at the base of the mountain where Moses received the Ten Commandments, around a chapel built by Constantine's mother, Helena, to cover what was believed to be the burning bush, sits the oldest continuously operating monastery in the world. Theodora's protection scheme would weather the spread of Islam, and her bishops would survive, but her endorsement had unforeseen consequences. The church remained divided after her death. Persecution of Miaphysites increased and the Coptic, Ethiopian, and Syrian church felt more and more oppressed by the Chalcedonians of Constantinople. When Islam spread in the 7th century, it felt easier and less risky to convert than remain a Miaphysite Christian in a Chalcedonian Empire.[30] In the end, Theodora contributed to the fracture of Christianity in the East.

---

30 A 7th century Coptic Bishop wrote how Miaphysites almost welcomed Muslim invasion because it meant more freedom than what they were experiencing in the Byzantine Empire. John, Bishop of

∽

For years, I needed Theodora to be a saint. I held her up as the first anti-human trafficker, the prostitute turned protector of the vulnerable. I needed her heroism, laughed at her cheekiness, and often imagined getting a tattoo of her monogram, but I was not ready to bear her mark on my body. *What if I find out things about her that I'm embarrassed by?* Even my hesitation was a sign of my own need to be all good, my unbearable feeling of failure.

The more I learn of Theodora, the more I read between the lines. The fact that Justinian stopped his tolerance of Miaphysites after her death makes me wonder how she exacted his compliance. That she sparred with Pope Silverius and defiantly protected eight bishops for twelve years is bold, brave, and also divisive. That multiple sources accuse her of manipulation, interference, subversion, and ambition also complicates matters. While it is true that strong women in history were sexualized and vilified in an attempt to erase or diminish their influence, it is also true that there is always more to the story. Where are they not wrong?

As I pilgrimage through Turkey now, I slowly come home to myself, unraveling messy narratives and shedding broken belief structures. I learn to hold the both/and of glory and depravity, power and harm, regret and impact. I am starting to welcome it, accepting its complexity, seeing its very real humanness, and calling it good. Theodora was all of those things. And if I let her be, I can let myself be also.

The women hear my story of Theodora, and as we weave our

Nikiu, *The Chronicle of John, Bishop of Nikiu*, trans. R. H. Charles (London: Oxford University Press, 1916), 144.

lives through the history and narrow streets, savoring the delicious food of our journey, she becomes a treasured symbol they associate with my story of becoming. Day after day, they come to find their own. Sometimes it's an experience, sometimes a place, often an a-ha moment from a dinner conversation. Each one ends up discovering her own treasured symbol.

Toward the end of the pilgrimage, I take them to an antique store like none other. The shopkeeper has been there for sixty years, and the little storefront is entirely covered with antiques, but in a highly organized fashion. In the front, blown glass lanterns, Turkish coffee pots, and tribal necklaces hang in bulk from the ceiling, and jewelry covers the walls. Glass cases are overflowing with rings, earrings, bracelets, and copper lighters. In the back are stacks of copper trays, old fez caps, and more vintage teapots, as well as hundreds of keys in various sizes and shapes. Up a narrow winding staircase full of old paintings, telephones, and typewriters is a tiny attic overflowing with everything else. It is a crazy, exhilarating treasure hunt. And that is what we're there to do.

In front of the store, on the floor beneath the hanging jewelry, are large bins full of antique coins. Thousands upon thousands of them. They have all sorts of metal discoloration, weight, and inscriptions, but they are old. And by old, I am talking about Roman—some are from the fourth century! The pilgrimage year I got my tattoo, these bins are what drew my attention. Could I possibly find a coin from Justinian and Theodora's reign?

As the women explored the rest of the store, I dug and sorted and started a collection on top of the glass case. Soon, a few others joined me, searching for their own symbolic coin. Eventually, I had three that the owner assured me depicted early

Byzantine rulers (on one side were two royal figures that looked like they could be an emperor and empress). But it wasn't until later that day, as we waited for our flight in the tiny regional airport, that someone showed me how to find things via Google Photos. We all excitedly confirmed it was indeed *them*!

I had discovered two tangible remnants of Theodora's reign during that trip, and would return with one tattooed on my arm and another to turn into a necklace and wear around my neck. God's gift to me, to remember. The work he continues to do in my life, inviting me back to myself, to my humanity, to my limitations and my glory, is symbolically represented in this woman from the sixth century.

Where have you known your own both/and: glory and depravity, power and harm, regret and impact? Have you come to embrace your own complex humanity? Why or why not?

KAHVALTI

A Turkish breakfast is a feast of opposites—a fitting symbol for Empress Theodora. Both savory and sweet adorn the table: olives of all colors, varieties of fresh cheeses, cucumber and tomato slices, hard-boiled eggs, slices of fried dried sausage, börek, and fresh bread accompanied by jams and honey. Of course, tea or Nescafé with milk is on hand in tiny cups, or cherry, peach, and apricot juice if that's your preference. The Turkish breakfast is a large weekend family affair dating back to the Ottomans. As the empire expanded, so did its exposure to food. The varied table of a Turkish breakfast harkens back to the lavish delicacies enjoyed by the sultan and palace. Today, families gather on Saturdays or Sundays for a leisurely brunch of all these foods and more.

MOSAICS

THEODORA'S MARK MAY be on the columns of the great Hagia Sophia, but there are also other women's faces gracing the walls of the upper gallery: Empress Zoe and Empress Irene. When I lived in Turkey, I never knew their names, let alone their stories. I never knew that the red-headed Empress Irene broke classism when she opened a hospital with five wards to treat every economic group in the city. Nor did I know the man pictured with Empress Zoe was the third face on the mosaic facade, changed each time she remarried, in the dramatic fashion that she did.

There's a resonance I experience in my not knowing. I reflect on the years I lived here—the multiple groups of people I brought to this building, appreciating the marble floor more than the stories behind these works of art, more than the women who shaped the place I called home. Their invisibility to me back then mirrors my own invisibility. I was a young mom on a male-led, Middle Eastern team of evangelicals. Any influence I had came via the position my husband held. It was honestly not hard to relate more to the marble floor than the gold tesserae on the wall.

❦

After the riots decimated the city, Justinian and Theodora rebuilt the present-day Hagia Sophia (it sits upon the ruins of two other churches) between 532 and 537 CE, for the equivalent of $462 million. Justinian is reputed to have said of its scale, "Solomon, I have vanquished thee." The columns upon which their monograms were carved were brought from the Temple of Artemis in Ephesus (one of the seven wonders of the world), and the dome was the largest in the world until St. Peter's Basilica was completed in 1626. For one thousand years, Christians worshiped here while the Emperor and Empress sat in the royal alcove above, until the last liturgy was held on May 28, 1453—the day before the city fell to the Ottomans and the church became a mosque.

When I lived in Istanbul, I could see the Hagia Sophia from across the Marmara Sea while sitting on our terrace. The four minarets flank the large dome, and the pink hue stands out from the gray skyline. To me, she served as a symbol of the faith that used to be preeminent in this land, and I mourned the minarets that were added when Constantinople fell to Islam. Back then, I had no idea that long before the Ottomans came, the city had already been weakened from within—by Christians themselves.

Two hundred years earlier, during the Fourth Crusade, the Venetians sacked the city, plundering some of the best Byzantine art and shipping it off to Europe. The four famous bronze horses that stand in the entryway to the Basilica of San Marco in Venice and the four tetrarchs that are built into the side of the same church, among other treasures, are all Byzantine. If not for this invasion and occupation, Constantinople, the last great city of Christian Byzantium, may have been strong enough two hundred years later in its defense against the Ottomans.

When the Ottomans came, they converted churches into mosques, added minarets, removed crosses, and covered images of humans. However, many of the mosaics depicting Jesus, Mary, and various emperors may have already been destroyed or covered up by either the Fourth Crusade or even before that, during Iconoclasm. The Hagia Sophia may have very well been in a constant state of repair and rediscovery during these centuries. For example, the oldest mosaic of Mary and Jesus above the altar was restored in 867 CE after the Seventh Ecumenical Council voted in favor of the use of icons in worship again. The newest mosaic, partially uncovered in the upper gallery, dates to the mid-thirteenth century, after the city was retaken from the invading Crusaders. The Ottomans covered all of the mosaics until Sultan Abdulmejid called for a restoration in the nineteenth century. This is when the church was painted with geometric designs, and gold-colored ceilings filled in the gaps left by broken and fallen gold tesserae.

As if she reflects the tune of the city, whose comings and goings she watches from the mouth of the Bosphorus, when the Ottoman Empire collapsed and the secularist Mustafa Kemal became president of the new Republic of Turkey, the Hagia Sophia was made into a museum. For nearly a century, visitors could get up close to the upper gallery mosaics, touch the Viking graffiti, grow sore from walking on the massive marble slabs, and imagine an altar in place of the Islamic Minbar. A mirror to the secular nationalist leanings of a young country, the Hagia Sophia was neither church nor mosque anymore.

And then, in 2020, as the pandemic ended tourism and the world was otherwise distracted, different leanings of a more conservative leader reverted the museum to a mosque. Green prayer rugs were laid over the huge marble slabs, shoe cubbies were installed, and disposable head coverings were provided. Two enormous sheets veiled the Mary and Jesus mosaic in the nave, and the upper gallery was closed to tourists.

UNESCO led the world in its outcry, but the President was immovable. The Hagia Sophia was once again an Islamic house of worship. The mosaics were again invisible; the stories they told hidden.

❧

For over twenty years, a pair of faux pink suede shoes has sat in their original box, with all the silica gel, in a storage container in our basement. Twenty years ago, they received about an hour and a half of use. Worn only once, but kept all these years because of the significance of the wearing.

Twenty years ago, I was smack in the middle of our time in Turkey. My husband was advancing in leadership, so we were invited to a massive regional conference on the coast at a gorgeous five-star hotel. There was going to be a banquet, and I, having recently lost baby weight, had purchased a brand-new outfit: a feminine, flowy, floral outfit with matching pink shoes.

When the hour of the banquet finally arrived, I nearly floated into the hall, feeling so lovely, so radiant. I sat with my four-year-old on one side and my one-year-old on the other at a table with six men. After the initial pleasantries and chit chat, the men dove into strategizing, posturing, and dominating. I became the wife, a mom, *invisible*.

Acutely aware of my feet in the faux pink suede shoes, hidden and unseen beneath the table, I tended to little children and excused ourselves an hour later, leaving my husband at the table full of men and their business.

I put the kids to bed, still wearing my shoes, so reluctant to remove them. Finally, as I slowly took off each article of newly bought clothing, making a pile of feminine pink on the dresser, I took off one shoe and then the next, putting them in their box, from which they never emerged again.

At the time, I wondered if there would ever be a day when I wouldn't resent my husband, my kids, or my organization for making me feel so unseen, for reducing me to a role instead of seeing me for who I am. My journal entry that night describes the chocolate I spent the evening eating, and then contains a list of holiday meal items and necessary office renovations. During our remaining time abroad, I would become the team chef and chief hostess, as in these roles, at least, I was visible.

Over the years, the pattern remains. That familiar feeling that I've sunk my entire heart into these efforts, wiggling beneath the table, just screaming to be seen, to be noticed for what they represent: *You are lovely in all your shed baby weight. You have offered us your truest self in these words. You ministered to us all in that talk. Thank you for thinking of us and for fostering a sense of community.* The situations are numerous and varied, but the feeling is a well-worn path in my soul: I desire to be truly noticed in a way that never feels satiated.

I am Zoe. I am Irene. You pass by me and leave with an overall feeling of goodness, but the stories you tell are full of the marble you walked upon, not the gold tesserae that sparkled above.

≈

Shockingly, in January of 2024, another change was made to the great Hagia Sophia. For four years, she had served as a mosque, free of charge to all visitors, even though the upstairs mosaics remained off-limits. I can only imagine how the loss of revenue from tourists impacted the upkeep of such an ancient building. The incredible increase in the number of visitors since 2020 (from 3.7 to 13.6 million in three years) caused wear and tear. And so, a hybrid solution was created: Muslim prayer-goers can enter the central apse and nave, while paying tourists can only enter the upstairs gallery. Now, visitors can pay a premium to come close to Irene and Zoe again, but can only look down upon the old sanctuary and see Theodora's monogram from above. It is both a loss and a gain.

In the mosaic, Empress Zoe (eleventh century) holds a scroll in her hands that reads "Most Pious Augusta." The irony is not lost on me—the woman next to the third-faced husband whose sixty-year-old skin looks so young because she was known for having an obsession with beauty and anti-aging concoctions, remembered as pious![31] Her acts as Empress include gouging out eyes, murder, and banishment to remote nunneries. It was a scandalous reign that concluded alongside her sister, Theodora (a different one).

Empress Irene (twelfth century) was also remembered for her piety and benevolence (the hospital and all) and is pictured next to her beloved son, who died of tuberculosis at age seventeen. Her husband's sister, Anna Komnene, tried to overthrow her brother and was exiled. While in exile, Anna wrote the most

------

31 Marios Panas, Effie Poulakou-Rebelakou, Nicolaos Kalfakis, and Dimitrios Vassilopoulos. "The Byzantine Empress Zoe Porphyrogenita and the Quest for Eternal Youth." *Journal of Cosmetic Dermatology* 11, no. 3 (2012): 245–248.

extensive history of the time, and is one of only two Byzantine female authors on record. The other, Kassiani (ninth century), wrote a hymn and has a cheeky story of her own.

For better or worse, notorious or benevolent, I choose to learn what we know of their stories, if for no other reason than I want mine remembered, too. If for no other reason than my mission is to make the unseen feminine seen. I search for their fingerprints to recognize my own. We were there, in this complicated city, and for a brief time, we left our mark. Theodora. Zoe. Irene. Beth.

Do you relate to feeling invisible? What are your metaphorical pink shoes?

İÇLI KÖFTE

These appetizers are my absolute favorite Turkish food. The words mean "stuffed meatball," and literally, it is flavorful minced meat inside a bulgur shell, fried. One is usually plenty and is typically served as a portion. But "içli" also refers to a person who is sensitive or keeps their emotions to themselves. As you contemplate feelings of being invisible, perhaps one of these crispy balls will be a good accompaniment. It's a time-consuming recipe, but worth it![32] I'll let you in on a secret: For a less tasty alternative, Trader Joe's sells frozen "kibbeh" that is close enough.

1. Soak 2 cups of fine bulgur and ½ cup of semolina flour in 1 ½ cups of hot water for 15 minutes.

2. Meanwhile, sauté 2 diced yellow onions in 2 tablespoons of olive oil and 2 tablespoons of butter. Add 400 grams of ground beef (or lamb, or a mix of the two).

3. Back to the bulgur mixture, add 1 teaspoon of salt, ½ cup of flour, 1 teaspoon of paprika, 1 teaspoon of tomato paste, 1 egg. Mix with a mixer until the mixture has the consistency of dough.

4. To the meat and onion mixture, add 1 teaspoon of chili flakes, 2 teaspoons of cumin, 1 teaspoon of pepper, a handful of chopped parsley, and ½ cup of chopped walnuts.

---

32 "İçli Köfte (Turkish Kibbeh) Recipe" *Turkish Style Cooking.* https:// turkishstylecooking.com/icli-kofte-turkish-kibbeh-recipe.html

5. With oiled hands, roll ⅓ cup of the dough into a ball and then hollow out the center. Place about 2 tablespoons of the meat into the center of the dough cavity, and then press the opening closed to obtain a lemon shape. Roll it around in your hands, making sure to seal and press the ends closed.

6. Freeze or refrigerate, and when you're ready to eat, deep-fry until golden brown.

CISTERNS

TRACY AND I cross the Bosphorus Strait via a steamer ferry that has been running nonstop for decades so I can show her my old neighborhood. Europe to Asia. Two continents split a city that has known more splits than I can count. On the hill above, the newest and biggest mosque is rivaled in height by the neighboring TV/Radio tower, the perfect symbol of Turkey's two competing religions: Islam and Secularism. It's her Centennial, and I've been watching her duality unfold for more than a quarter century.

As I mentioned earlier, my old "neighborhood" was ancient Chalcedon, the site of the Fourth Ecumenical Council, held in 451 CE, convened by Empress Pulcheria and attended by over 500 bishops, to settle once and for all the two distinct natures of God the Father and God the Son. Nothing remains above ground from the fifth century, unless you count the ancient fish market and smell of roasting chestnuts. We walk the cobblestone streets, and memories bombard me—not just the assault on my husband or the hospital we frequented or the stress of driving the sole thoroughfare, but also the lovely view from *that* terrace and the ice cream shop on *that* corner and playing in the kiddie pool on *that* roof.

In a country defined by the division of two, I'm learning to add. I may be here to lead a group of women, but there is always something specific for me in my return: a new theme, another layer, a shift in perspective. Turkey has always been the place where God gets my attention, and the year we walk these streets, the theme has to do with embracing both/and, the complex humanity of the lost women we're discovering. Because in truth, I've been lost, too.

I "grew up" in this divided place: became a mom, learned to mentor, and celebrated our tenth wedding anniversary. And also, I traveled well-worn paths of a bifurcated soul. I learned to distance myself from my weakness rather than welcome her home, draw her close, or tend to her well.

Over the past few years, as I've discovered other women who left their fingerprints on the history of this place, I have mined all the ways to celebrate them and augment their impact. Only recently have I realized my propensity to do to these women what the church did when it canonized them as saints. In their veneration, we dismiss their humanity. In praising their sanctity, virginity, miracles, or martyrdom, we *other* them. They cannot be like us with gold halos and stories of resurrection.

In my study of addition, I'm learning to embrace both as true: strength and weakness, honor and shame, beauty and harm. And when I allow both to be true of Pulcheria, Theodora, Macrina, or Priscilla, they both get to be true of me, too. The both/and. The complexity of being human, not a saint.

It's incredible how much these ancient women teach me about myself—how much they heal me, mending the shattered bits that first landed me in this country. Strength and determination, faith and hope led me here. But dashed dreams and chaos and daily trauma nearly tore me in two. I had to lean into the former to survive, and now every trip back returns more of me to myself.

I welcome her like a younger friend. I receive the mend on another tear I forgot was there. A new theme. A newly discovered woman from the past. A different guide who has more for me to find. I come a little more home to myself, knowing now there will be more to come, next time.

This time, I'm telling a more well-rounded story. I'll let Empress Pulcheria guide me.[33]

After a long, hot morning and an equally hot lunch, we turn off the ancient Divan Yolu and walk one block to a modern glass building. It sticks out incongruently in this ancient part of the city; perhaps the odd triangular shape is a nod to this reality. As we wait for our timed entrance, I reveal what it is we stand upon.

In 2010, during the demolition of a government administrative building, as is common in Istanbul, ruins were discovered. All work halted until a historical review committee could assess the find, and the results were astonishing. Not only did they find one of the suspected 200-plus Byzantine cisterns, but it was one of the oldest, entirely intact examples of the complex water system of the ancient world. They dated this particular cistern to the fifth century, when the Emperor Theodosius II built the walls around Constantinople, collected all of the laws that had been passed in the one hundred years since Constantine, and rebuilt the Hagia Sophia (the second of the three versions). A Roman aqueduct already existed nearby, bringing fresh water

---

33 Adapted from author's original post "Coming Home to Myself," *Red Tent Living*, November 2023.

from northern springs, and cisterns served as underground storage tanks. Marble columns (in this case, thirty-two) were pillaged from Greek ruins and used to hold up the thirty-foot-high ceiling. Reopened in 2018, this cistern provides a reprieve from the bustling streets above, where visitors can enjoy a laser light show projected onto its columns and walls.

Cisterns were to the ancient world what dams, water treatment plants, and water towers are to ours. In other words, they served as reservoirs for the entire neighborhood. However, unlike the concrete slabs of dams or the rusty metal of large tanks, cisterns were architectural marvels, fittingly referred to as palaces in Turkish. Beneath the ground, rows of marble columns held up red brick domes, smaller versions of the domed churches built above ground. Today, you can enjoy fine dining in the Sarnıç cistern, a jazz concert in the Yerebatan cistern, and see Tom Hanks stop a virus from being released in one in the movie *Inferno*. If you look carefully, you'll walk right over a slight swelling in the sidewalk in the first courtyard of the Topkapı Palace, built on top of a Byzantine cistern.

However, I have not led us to the Theodosius II cistern to discuss water. There is a far more interesting story connected to the man who built this underground palace. For long before Theodosius II ruled, his older sister, Pulcheria, served as his regent. They were orphaned at the ages of seven and ten, and Pulcheria was declared Augusta (Empress) when she turned fifteen. Her influence over her brother's reign, his future marriage, and the fate of Christendom cannot be overstated. I am not a historian, have not read all of the early Church Fathers' writings, and struggle to fully appreciate the nuances debated at each of the church councils. What follows is my synthesis and exegesis of the narrative through Pulcheria's lens. In other words, this is how I construct the story, to the best of my ability.

It was the early 400s, and the theological golden age for women was waning. Regional church councils were chipping away at female influence. The Council of Laodicea decided women could no longer enter the sanctuary or be ordained in 363 CE. The Council of Nimes revoked the priesthood of women in 394 CE. The Council of Carthage outlined restrictive instructions for how women could baptize and disciple in 398 CE.

As official roles and influence for women within the church shrank throughout the fourth century, another form of piety and leadership arose: monasticism.[34] Desert mothers in Egypt and female-led monastic communities in central Turkey drew women who wanted control of their faith expression, and arguably more control over their bodies.[35] Rebuffing Roman cultural norms (and laws) of marriage and the inherent danger of childbirth, women took vows of chastity and devoted themselves to Christ.

Pulcheria took such a vow of virginity and compelled her two younger sisters to do the same. However, hers was not a private vow, but a public ceremony at a church in which she

---

34 After Constantine made Christianity legal (Edict of Milan, 313 CE), martyrdom was replaced by asceticism as the purest expression of holiness. As the church came out of the shadows and defined liturgical structures in various church councils, women found new places of leadership within monastic communities.

35 Some notable women were Sarah, Theodora, and Syncletica in Egypt and Macrina, Nonna, and Gorgonia in Cappadocia.

linked the success of her brother's reign to her virginity.[36] The connection between imperial and theological rule started when her grandfather, Theodosius I, declared Nicene Christianity the empire's sole legal religion.[37] From then on, the royal family ruled by divine right. With the title of Empress and the status of a virgin, Pulcheria wielded power unlike most women of the time.

In the midst of this climate, the heated debate around the nature of the Virgin Mary ignited. Mary was becoming a bigger deal as the "Cult of Virginity" grew. She had become the virgin of virgins and a symbol to women of all classes. However, by the early fifth century, only the church in Ephesus was dedicated to her (compared to the thousands that exist today), probably because the Ephesians had replaced their worship of the virgin Artemis with that of the Virgin Mary. More on that later.[38]

At the time, the patriarch of Constantinople, second in power only to the pope in Rome, was Nestorius. He served as the Emperor's priest and wielded significant theological influence. He and Pulcheria had a run-in at Saint Irene Church, where he reportedly blocked her from entering the Holy of Holies to receive the Eucharist, an act only God's representative (a.k.a., the Emperor) could do. She reportedly said, "Have I not given birth to God?" likely aligning herself with the

---

36 History with Zea, "The Teenage Girl That Changed the Christian Religion | Aelia Pulcheria," YouTube video, 12:34, https://www.youtube.com/watch?v=Gz0M0bcpVM4.

37 Meaning, the doctrine agreed upon at the Nicean Church Council in 325 CE was declared orthodox.

38 The Cult of Mary is also known as the Marian Cult and represents the emphasis on the holiness of virginity.

Virgin Mary and declaring her own holiness. After this incident, Nestorius intensified the theological debate surrounding the nature of the Virgin Mary. Did Pulcheria's power threaten him? Was he a misogynist? What motivated the intensity of his argument that Mary was not *Theotokos* (mother of God), but *Christokos* (mother of Jesus, the man)?

Opposing Nestorius was Bishop Cyril of Alexandria. In 430 CE, Cyril sent letters to Pulcheria as well as to the Empress Eudocia, Theodosius II's wife, outlining his arguments for Theotokos. Surely he knew he was further inciting division among the two most influential women in the palace, who stood on opposite sides of this debate. To solve the argument, and perhaps to placate the women in his life, Theodosius II convened the Third Ecumenical Council and, to appease his sister, agreed it would be held in Ephesus at the Church of Saint Mary.[39]

When ecumenical councils were convened, all bishops were required to attend, including those from Rome, Carthage, Alexandria, Antioch, and Constantinople. Over 200 representatives attended the Council of Ephesus in 431 CE, but they didn't all arrive at the same time. Before all contingents appeared, Cyril launched into the debate which eventually led to a decision that Mary was indeed Theotokos, mother of God. Cyril wrote, "There was much joy and lighting of lights in the city, so that even women carrying censors led the way for us."[40] (Women carried the incense-burning censors of the priesthood!)

---

39 "The Development of the 'Nestorian Controversy (through A.D. 429)", *Fourth-Century Christianity*, https://www.fourthcentury.com/narrative-of-the-christological-controversies/

40 Atanassova, Antonia. 2011. "Orthodox Women's Defense of the Theotokos: The Case of Empress Pulcheria and the Council of

So, Pulcheria won. The Virgin Mary's importance was cemented. In the streets of Constantinople, people chanted, "Mary the Virgin has deposed Nestorius! Many years to Pulcheria! She is the one who has strengthened the faith!"[41] Pulcheria went on to build three churches in Constantinople dedicated to Mary, among other significant philanthropic buildings. But the Council's decision had unwittingly exposed another theological debate: If Mary was the mother of God, then was Jesus fully man *and* fully God in her womb? How were they to understand and explain the nature of Christ? They needed another council!

Tired of the whole thing, Theodosius II refused to convene another council. But a year after his death, having stepped back into the authority of the Empress (Theodosius' wife, Eudocia, was on pilgrimage/exile in Jerusalem), Pulcheria did just that. In 451 CE, just across the Bosphorus in my old neighborhood, Kadıköy, the Fourth Ecumenical Council gathered to decide the nature of Christ. Where Nestorius had proclaimed complete separation of Jesus' humanity and deity, the pendulum swung in the opposite direction, led by a revered monk named Eutyches. He argued that after the incarnation, Jesus' humanity was extinguished and entirely subsumed (or absorbed) by his deity.[42] The Council of Chalcedon debated and decided on the doctrine we hold to be orthodox today: Jesus is both fully man and fully divine, comprising two natures in one person. And

---

Ephesus." *Sophia Institute Studies in Orthodox Theology* 2. September 13. Columbia University Academic Commons. https://academiccommons.columbia.edu/doi/10.7916/D8RV0Z2Z

41 Ibid.

42 This belief was known as Monophytism and declared heresy.

presiding over the final session was Empress Pulcheria. Pope Leo wrote Pulcheria that year "that both the Nestorian and Eutychian heresies had been overcome largely by her efforts."[43]

We have all heard of the results of these councils, that Mary is the mother of God, who is both fully God and fully man. But who has heard of Pulcheria, the woman behind our faith? The lost woman of Christendom?

The first time I tell her story atop the cistern her brother built, I'm still unaware of the breadth of her role. I have yet to discover the intricacies of the theological debates she led, nor do I realize her fingerprints reach to Ephesus, where we'll conclude our pilgrimage. The previous day, we walked by the Saint Irene Church, and I hadn't yet made the connection that the incident with her and Nestorius had happened *there.* The magnitude of the feminine in this city, this land, is endless. It overwhelms and excites, offering a perennial treasure hunt.

And for all that I have since learned about Pulcheria's role in church history, there will be more to come after this trip. I will also learn of abuses of her power, the oddity of the Marian Cult, and the unforeseen consequences of a century of virgins. I will learn that the church in which the fourth council met was named after another woman whose relics miraculously helped sway the decision. The difference is that I am ready for the complexity. I am ready to absorb the fallenness of these women into their glory. I expect it. I allow them to be both women who

---

43 "St. Pulcheria," *The Catholic Encyclopedia*, New Advent, https://www.newadvent.org/cathen/12561c.htm.

brought forth good and women who brought forth harm—to be human, just like they fought for the right of their savior to be.

Queens and virgins: the women of history who seem to find some modicum of power or voice. Just like Istanbul is divided into two continents and this country embraces two religions (Islam and Secularism), we are left with the both/and of the female. Our legacy will be the unforeseen consequences of our humanity and the beautiful work we do as image bearers.

I have no way of knowing the year Tracy and I wander through my old neighborhood, the year I return as CEO of our business, that I will navigate this very thing. I will lead the organization through changes that have staggering consequences for all of us. It will be good and lonely and devastating and hopeful, all within 365 days. I will return one year later, and God will use other metaphors to speak to me, and he will remind me of Pulcheria. I will remark how proud I am of how strong I've become, and also, the women will notice how weary and bruised I am.

Becoming noticeable, visible, and leading with, not behind, my husband will be both glorious and dangerous. As women, we know this in a more embodied way. We may not take vows of chastity to own it, but the wear and tear on our souls is felt deeply. We are watched and judged and suspected and also praised and consumed and demanded. It will be a whiplash year. By the time I get to the sea, the water will come for me in a whole new way. The song lyrics, "Somehow this sorrow is shaping my heart like it should," become a refrain of that pilgrimage.[44] My Byzantine sisters will welcome me home.

---

44 Andrew Peterson, *Always Good*, Track 11 on *Light for the Lost Boy* (Centricity Music, 2012), Spotify, https://open.spotify.com/track/6GgHFLUXNOJKKeYlz4x5YA.

> *Who is a "Pulcheria" for you? Who does God use to remind you of your image-bearing?*

ECUMENICAL CHURCH COUNCILS & HIGHLIGHTS:

First: 325 AD Nicea

Debated Arianism (divinity of Jesus), the doctrine of the Trinity, Jesus begotten, Father and Son of one essence.

Second: 381 AD Constantinople

Debated the Holy Spirit, defeated Arianism, decided the Trinity is three persons in one essence Homoousia).

Third: 431 AD Ephesus

Defeated Nestorianism: the belief that Jesus is Man and God as two separate persons and Mary is therefore Christokos (Christ-bearer). Decided Mary is Theotokos (God-bearer).

Fourth: 451 AD Chalcedon

Debated Monophysitism, the belief that Jesus is Man and God subsumed him (like sugar cube in water) and is now 100% divine. Adopted Dyophysitism: Jesus has two distinct natures in one person - hypostasis (essence of both).

Fifth: 553 AD Constantinople

Continued to debate Monophysitism and Miaphysitism, the belief that Jesus is Man and God in one nature, and confirmed the Council of Chalcedon's position on Jesus' two distinct natures.

Sixth: 680 AD Constantinople

Debated if Jesus had two wills or one.

Seventh: 787 AD Nicea

Debated and decided that icons were wrong (Iconoclasm).

EZO GELIN ÇORBASI

In the early twentieth century, a young woman named Zöhre lived in the southeastern part of Turkey. She was matched, married, and mistreated by her first husband and then allowed (or maybe forced) to divorce. Her father arranged for her to marry a relative from a village across the border, and to gain approval from her soon-to-be mother-in-law, Zöhre (also known as Ezo), prepared a soup to impress: the bride Ezo's soup, aka Ezo Gelin Çorbası. She and her new husband stayed in Syria and had nine children, but she died depressed at a young age. Her story is a legend. The Turks have created songs and television series about her and even repatriated her remains in 1999. Then, in 2013, her 71-year-old *daughter* escaped from Syria with six of her nine children and asked to stay in her mother's hometown! Welcome home, Ezo's family!

This soup is cozy, filling, and easy to make. The secret is the red lentils. If you have a Middle Eastern grocer or a bulk section that sells thin red lentils, they work better. Here is an excellent recipe for you to try and honor Ezo, the sad bride.[45]

1. Sauté 1 diced yellow onion in 1 tablespoon oil and 1 tablespoon butter.

2. Stir in 1 tablespoon of tomato paste, 1 teaspoon of flour, and 1 teaspoon of paprika.

3. Add 7 cups of water and bring to a boil.

---

45 "Ezogelin Soup Recipe," *Turkish Style Cooking*, https://turkishstylecooking.com/ezogelin-soup-recipe.html

4. Add ¼ cup rice, red lentils, and bulgur, and cook with a lid until they are softened.

5. Serve with mint sprinkled on top. Salt to taste.

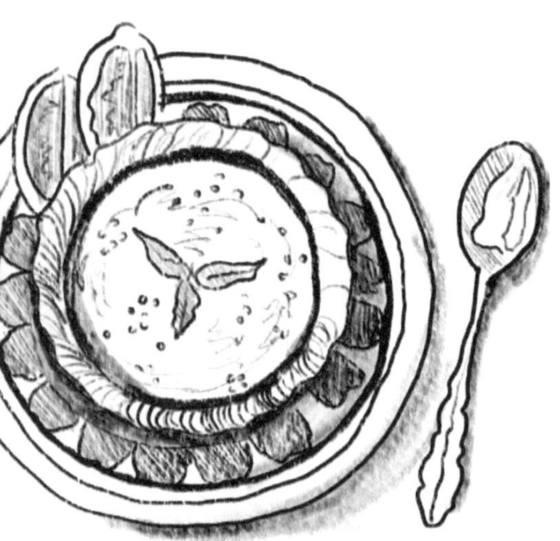

MINARETS

BEFORE EACH TRIP begins, on my first night back in Istanbul, I like to go to a restaurant whose rooftop lies between the Hagia Sophia and the Blue Mosque. Inevitably, at some point in the meal, the last Call to Prayer of the day loudly reverberates from the many minarets in the area, welcoming me back to my old home. Since the Hagia Sophia was reverted to a mosque in 2020, the last Call to Prayer of the day, the Isha, is chanted as a duet between the muezzins (prayer chanters) of these two mosques. It is beautiful and haunting, a breathtaking entrance into our pilgrimage.

A few nights later, we lead the women to the park benches in between these two mosques, Turkish desserts in hand to augment the decadent two days of food, history, and story. We have looked it up: the Isha is at 8:38 p.m. tonight. We have thirty minutes to discuss the metaphor these two mammoth buildings illustrate.[46] On our left is the Hagia Sophia, a symbol of Christianity, the Byzantine Empire, and God's promise to Sarah. On our right is the Blue Mosque, a symbol of Islam, the Ottoman Empire, and God's promise to Hagar.

---

46 Metaphor reframes our experience by inviting our imagination to reinterpret our thoughts, feelings, and the meanings we have made.

It is the story of two women, and the impossible position they found themselves in. We talk about envy's power to destroy you from the inside and the devastation when you are the subject of another's envy. The assortment of baklava gets passed around, and we shoo the cats away as we grapple with the legacy on either side of us: Sarah's son, Isaac and Hagar's son, Ishmael, and the centuries-long grief between the two.[47]

And then the Blue Mosque muezzin begins:

Allah is the greatest
I testify that there is no god but Allah
I testify that Muhammad is the messenger of Allah
Come to the prayer
Come to success
Allah is the greatest
There is no god but Allah

Back and forth they chant as we silently take it in. Later, the vocalist among us will point out how crisp and clear the Hagia Sophia muezzin sounded compared to the minor key of the one from the Blue Mosque. Is it a biased perspective that minor keys in our tonal range are reserved for lament? A subconscious association with Islam? Maybe. I allow for Christians, new to a Muslim-majority land, to sit with the disruption and discomfort they first experience during the Call to Prayer. Of anyone, I can relate.

---

47 It's worth noting that when she abused Hagar, Sarah was still called Sarai. Additionally, we do not know Hagar's Egyptian name, but the Hebrew version was a dismissive for "outsider" or "foreigner."

Earlier, as I had walked up the congested hill toward the great church, I stopped to ask a carpet salesman the meaning of the string of lights between the minarets of the Hagia Sophia: "La ilaha illallah: There is no god truly worthy of worship except Allah." I'm still discovering many simple things I was too afraid to learn when I lived here.

A combination of my age, the stage of my faith, and the nature of our work led to very black-and-white thinking back then. If Christians weren't right and Muslims weren't wrong, why was I living on the other side of the world from loving and helpful grandparents? Watching my toddler climb high on the monkey bars while all the Turkish nannies scolded me that he would fall, shaming me with their 'tsk tsk,' I *needed* to be right. I could endure the loneliness of cross-cultural parenting if we were right. Not only the hardships of parenting abroad, but everything else as well. Everything was "endurable" if we were *right*. It made all that was hard worth it. I couldn't survive *and* hold space for nuance.

And so I didn't ask. *What do the words strung up in lights on the Hagia Sophia mean? What is the muezzin saying five times a day, every day? What is it really like for the women who pray in the small, private alcoves of the mosques designated just for them? How do the women get all of their hair to stay tucked away beneath their silk scarves?* These are the things I have asked about and learned *since*. Since the spaciousness in me grew. Since gray became a favorite color. Since curiosity became a friend, I buried the need for certainty.

Back then, I would have used words like "dark" and "evil" and "sad" to describe the feeling of sitting between these two sets of minarets. The American church sent us to "save the lost," and co-workers talked about the heaviness that descended (or lifted) upon entering and leaving this Muslim country. For a moment, the only melancholy I feel is for all that I missed in my lack of curiosity. No Theodora. No Zoe or Irene. No Kösem, and certainly none of the complexity of Sarah and Hagar's legacy.

⁂

Envy is a scary word for women. One of those things we've all known, but are deeply ashamed of, if we've ever named it at all. We've been confronted by it for two days—in the harem, in the hamam, and by now among each other's stories. Spend enough time in the company of women, and envy will surface. As the stories start to unfold, none of us travels far before we stumble upon being the object of another woman's envy or the perpetrator ourselves. Oh, and it's such a well-worn, tired tale. Our mother Eve was envy's first victim, and women have had a unique relationship with it ever since.

I have become intimately acquainted with envy's mark and lost friendships as a result. I often feel that I am the object of parental and marital envy. Usually, I don't even share about my family with women; so unsafe are the waters if all things are well in comparison to theirs. Although I wrote a book about parenting, I no longer discuss it. But I, too, envy. My heart envies most what it lacks: the ease of business, the growth of a platform, success in publishing. Envy leads to contempt, and in this regard, I am both victim and perpetrator.

The Call to Prayer has ended, and we resume our discussion. Sarah and Hagar were in an impossible position: a barren woman with the burden of bringing forth Abraham's prophetic promise in a culture where polygamy was the norm. Sarah must have been resentful of her limited choices long before Hagar conceived. And Hagar, resentful of being made a concubine and then subject to her mistress's subsequent abuse. One woman envious of a womb, the other envious of honor.

The women of our group ponder their mothers, sisters, and friends. They consider anew if their lived experience could be attributed to envy. The unexplained bitterness or harsh treatment or perceived abandonment they've been on the receiving end of—all attributable to envy? As in, maybe they aren't a bad daughter, disappointing sister, or selfish friend? Envy takes on flesh as we sit with a reframed narrative for a few minutes.

I smile as I imagine Hagar stumbling up to the spring on the road to Shur, weary and thirsty from a long day of desert walking. She is ticked. Grumbling to herself, she rails against patriarchy, polygamy, the sexualization of women, and the old patriarch's god for giving a promise his own wife couldn't fulfill. And then! Though she conceived, she remained a servant while Sarah kept her esteemed position, only with even more venom for her servant girl. Hagar is muttering as she draws water from the spring, unaware of the man nearby. And in my mind, this man, whom early theologians believed was pre-incarnate Christ, is smiling, holding back a chuckle, as he listens to her.[48] Of course, Jesus would make an appearance at the dawn of the Abrahamic Covenant! But to appear to the mother of Ishmael? The mother of Arabs, not his own lineage?

He appears after envy between the two women led to rupture. Hagar has left. And God has *seen* her. He knows. And he allows her to be the first to name him—*the God who Sees.*

---

48 Genesis 16:7-15 uses "angel of the Lord." Tertullian (2nd century), Origin (3rd century), and Augustine (5th century) all argue the "angel of the Lord" in the Old Testament is the pre-incarnate Logos or Christ.

The God who sees patriarchy.
The God who sees sexualization.
The God who sees unfairness.
The God who sees envy.

And he is the one who sees and *still* treats her equally, giving her the same promise as Abraham received. She, too, will have descendants too numerous to count. Equal to Sarah as a mother of generations and equal to Abraham, too. The matriarch to the patriarch.

Equality will be our theme on the pilgrimage as I guide us back in time to greater and greater female voice, presence, and leadership. We started in the seventeenth-century Ottoman Empire and entered the Byzantine centuries between 325 and 1453 CE. In Cappadocia, we'll be in the fourth century, alongside early church mothers, and by the time we arrive in Ephesus, we'll be in the first century. This method of gliding backward in time through the stories of women paints a haunting picture of the silencing of the feminine, which increased over time.

But for now, Hagar. I am stunned as I realize the promise given to her, in such a similar language, was a statement of worth and value, elevating her to the same level as the promise given to Abraham. Of course, the story of the feminine predates Paul and the incarnate Jesus (which will be our theme in Ephesus)! Why am I surprised? This is the story that has slowly been unfolding for me.

❧

I have a theory I'm working on that I'll allude to with the group in the following two cities we visit. But this interlude, this transition evening in the park (the next morning we'll fly to the middle of the country), dips into it in a way that makes my body hum. Adrenaline is pulsing as I sit there in the warm evening darkness, the mosques lit up beautifully, families strolling in between, and mangy cats playing. Thinking about Hagar in this way is not new to me, but there's something new in that scene I imagined: where she's pissed and Jesus is there smirking, on the desert road to Shur. It's the dawn of the covenant, the time period, that gets me. Lately, I've been intrigued by women and time.

We purposefully begin in Istanbul, visiting places from the Ottoman period, and discussing the Sultanate of Women in all its ostensible invisibility. By the sixteenth century, notable women made it to the pages of history, but only barely, and vis-à-vis a man. However, as we travel backward in time, into the annals of Byzantium, we encounter women like Theodora, Pulcheria, and Zoe. And as we go back further still, we see more and more women leading, writing, and preaching. In fact, the first century offered women more equality than any other in the last two millennia.

And here is where my body is humming: Whenever we see Jesus show up, we see genderism shattered. It would be enough to say *it started with Hagar*, but I wonder. Did it? Or did it start at the very beginning? Did it begin with Eve? Was He there, too?

✦

The disruptive evening in the park, with its setting and topic of envy, is the perfect end to two days in Istanbul. The exotic sites, smells, and sounds; the sensory invitation in the hamam and the discomfort in the harem; the way we've engaged around the dinner table, which is starting to surface all of our stories, is an exceptionally curated entry to our pilgrimage.

We must first leave behind our routine, our norms, and our lived reality to discover what we've always known to be true about who we are. To achieve this requires more than a plane ride across the ocean; to obtain quicker results than a ten-day trip allows, it is best to strip away the coping mechanisms and outer self abruptly. There is truly no better place to do so than Istanbul.

We are on the *Lost Women of Turkey Pilgrimage*, but the women on the trip still don't quite realize they, too, are lost. Or have been. For aren't we all, always, out of touch with some parts of our soul? Aren't we always on a journey of recovery, rediscovery, rewriting, and retelling? That's why each time I return, a new theme emerges. As much as my story is alive, I find new ways to locate it in the metaphors of this land.

Macrina Weirderkehr writes, "Jesus always wants to resurrect us. The fact that something isn't visible does not mean it isn't present. It may be very near—waiting to be discovered."[49] Istanbul removes a layer or two, allowing us to hear a little differently. By the time we leave, we each have a sense that there is something *very near*. Perhaps all of our bodies are humming with the sensation of something about to be discovered.

> *When you experience disruption or discomfort, how does your body respond? How might you choose a different response next time? How can you make space for curiosity?*

---

49 Macrina Wiederkehr, *Behold Your Life: A Pilgrimage Through Your Memories* (Notre Dame, IN: Sorin Books, 2000), 15.

BAKLAVA

This dessert dates back to the eighth century BCE but gained popularity in the early 1500s in the Ottoman Empire. One of the few desserts that crossed religious lines, each year the sultan would gift a tray to each of his soldiers during the Baklava Procession. Christian Ottomans would use it in Lent, and Jewish Ottomans would use it to celebrate Purim. The fifth-generation baklava store in Istanbul is across the Golden Horn, and their pistachio and walnut version is sublime. As you consider the legacy of Sarah and Hagar, enjoy a dessert that has become part of both faiths' traditions.

1. Baklava is easier to make than you might think. You'll need phyllo dough, walnuts, sugar, cinnamon, and a lemon.

2. In a food processor, combine 4 cups of walnuts and 1 tablespoon of cinnamon, and pulse until the walnuts are ground.

3. Using a 9"x13" baking dish, brush one phyllo sheet with melted butter (you'll use about 1 cup of butter), layering 9 times, then cover with walnuts. Repeat with one more set of 9, and then use at least 5 sheets of phyllo for the final top layer.

4. Bake until golden brown at 350 degrees. Meanwhile, boil 1 cup of sugar in ¾ cup of water with 2 tablespoons of lemon juice. Let cool.

5. Remove the baklava from the oven and pour the

syrup on top, letting it soak in. When cool, cut into squares and then triangular slices. Sprinkle with ground pistachios.

PART 3

CAPPADOCIA: WORSHIPING IN CAVES

4TH CENTURY

THE PILGRIM'S BODY and soul emerge from the first stage of transformation, stripped down and weary, primed for what God has in store for them. They are a little closer to the new and old places of the heart, just days earlier buried beneath survival strategies and callous hardening. We have entered the metaphorical desert: a place where, in the soul's desolation, we might be seen at a well, offered living water, admonished to return to the difficulty of life with a new perspective, or at least a promise. The dry, arid climate of Cappadocia and the limestone landscape from which our hotel is carved form the backdrop. The living history of cave churches, hiding places, and unknown females immortalized in frescoed walls invites us to consider our own lives: Where do we hide? Where have we known dehumanization? Where are we parched?

This is why I wake early to capture the magic of 150 hot air balloons and allow the rising sun to warm my cheeks. It is my thin place, primarily because I started my journey in Istanbul and the stripping has already succeeded. I am weary. I am weak. I am ready to receive. Have at it, Lord. What do you have for me this year?

In ancient times, the people here worshiped a goddess. Her statue has been uncovered in nearby Çatalhöyük: a large-breasted woman, mid-birth, flanked by two felines, dated 8,000 years old. Thousands of small female figurines have been discovered throughout the area. The town we'll visit for a pottery demonstration was called *Queen,* and before that, *Mother Goddess* in the local language. The year we see a replica of the 8,000-year-old statue in front of a pottery studio, I have been mulling over God as mother. As I've entered into a new season of my own motherhood, I am in need of *her* in ways I've never experienced.

We are now in the fourth century on our journey of discovering the lost women of Turkey. Where we encountered women with titles in Byzantium, in the caves of the desert, we will find another sort of woman. These women utilized the currency of their bodies rather than the currency of power, and led in more publicly sanctioned ways than their sisters would just one hundred years later. As we move further back in time, we encounter a church not as removed from the revolutionary Jesus and not as tainted by empire. She still remembers and has much to teach us.

CAVES

We are picked up at our cave hotel in a party bus. LED lights flicker between red and blue as American pop music blares from the radio. Ten minutes later, we are dropped off in front of a regal cave restaurant entrance for a Turkish folk dance show and escorted down a long hallway to a vaulted cave room. Turkish meze (appetizers) and fresh bread await us at our long table, and waiters are not far behind to take our orders. We enjoy eggplant salad, yogurt with dill, hummus, a feta-filled pastry, and carrot salad. For the main, we choose between the regional specialty Tepebaşı (stew simmered in a clay pot) or köfte (spiced meatballs). Local wines and Rakı (licorice liquor) are self-serve at the end of the table. It is good that the party bus returns us to our hotel.

The food and drink are not the reason we have come, however. As the last of the tables fill in the alcoves that fan around the center stage, the lights dim, and drums start. The show has begun. A dance troupe of four men and four women put on a dazzling performance of folk dances from Anatolia, the heartland of Turkey. They perform high-energy choreographies in elaborate costumes, then quickly change and reappear. We see a proposal skit, a wedding dance, and a knife-throwing competition, as well as various regional dances, as they entertain the audience. There are attempts to include the guests, and during the more complicated costume changes, the disco light flashes and pop music roars as tourists are pulled from their tables.

Our party gasps when the most reserved among us is the first to jump up and dance with abandon. Later, she will share how freeing it was to be so uncontained. I am always more sheepish than I'd like to be, afraid that my klutzy movements will embarrass me. One day, I will be the first to rise. But it is not today, not yet.

After the meze and main course and more wine, after the wedding dance and knives and whirling dervish, the room goes dark and the belly dancer appears, waving her winged cape as it turns colors and shapes in her spinning. The room goes wild. Our table grows uncomfortable.

I remember how conflicted I felt the first time I saw a belly dancer. We were at a staff dinner in a hotel restaurant in a different Turkish city. As dessert plates were removed, the live music picked up a beat, and the dancer came into the center of the room. Our Turkish staff, men and women, stood to clap along. It was disorienting to see men who wore vestments at church egging on a half-clothed woman. Equally strange was that the female audience seemed just as delighted. I came to understand better (and mildly appreciate) the cultural norm of this ancient dance, but it never ceased to be a provocative show for me.

No one knows for sure where belly dancing originated, whether in Turkey, India, Egypt, or all three. Was it a fertility dance, wedding performance, or both? We know it was highly popular in the sultan's harem, though how it was entirely accepted in Islamic culture eludes me. Surprisingly, today, America is the country with the highest number of belly dancers in the world as women learn the art for personal empowerment.

The belly dancer at the cave restaurant continues as guests approach her and tuck cash beneath her top strap. It is this act that resembles a strip club, and the sexual objectification is too much for some of us. Bathroom breaks ensue. I sit quietly, observing the belly dancer through the women's eyes. How do we appreciate the female body and all it can do without commodifying it? How can the dance be both empowering and highly skilled, yet not require consumption? Can we separate historic and cultural from our modern-day reference points?

The whole thing lasts too long, and then she pulls up to the stage three awkward male tourists. In an attempt to entertain us all, she tries to teach them the undulating belly moves. Of course, they look ridiculous, and we can't help but laugh as she humiliates them. When shame becomes her abuse of power, I am done. Shame begets shame, and therefore, I can't help but conclude that her dance is not just an artistic folk dance she takes pride in performing, but one in which she is grossly objectified.

The night is a little tainted as we board the party bus, forced to hold the layers of history, culture, and femininity. The unfamiliar and uncomfortable bring it to the forefront in ways we cannot easily ignore, but there is a palpable recognition of a universal complexity.

In the States, the discourse of femininity centers on similar themes these days: When is a woman's body free and empowered, and when is it co-opted and objectified? In the anti-human trafficking movement, I hear it debated among sex workers, some proudly claiming power and agency over their bodies. In the courts, it's being discussed state by state in a post-Roe v. Wade era. In homes with teen girls, it's discussed in terms of modesty.

Our group of women captured this complexity well: On one end of the spectrum, a contained woman experienced freedom, an abandon to the music and her body in a way that felt truly holy. At the other end, a woman with her own stories felt triggered and angered by the dancer's objectification. We return to our cave hotel, fully aware that holding the varied and storied parts of the feminine feels heavy and sacred.

More was at play in that cave than what we experienced, as is the case in all Cappadocian caves.

There are Sundays when I stay home, nursing a third cup of coffee, and long for another time—a specific moment, to be precise, when I understood what the mystics meant when they talk of a thin space. Nearly twenty years ago now, I still choose to remember the taste of heaven it offered. I allow my thoughts to drift as I search Spotify for an approximation of what my soul remembers it heard.

Our staff team had gathered in Cappadocia for a retreat, and after a couple of days of meetings, one of the local staff led a hike through a valley of soft rock formations and ancient hermitages. The air was crisp and the path challenging as we traversed fallen boulders and thick tree roots. Our four-year-old was far ahead, trailing behind the staff member he most adored. Murat, our trail guide, was a small man with a big smile.[50] A pastor and evangelist, he was also the senior staff member among us. After about an hour, he paused the group and scaled the valley wall, entering a hole a good seven feet above ground. A minute later, his smiling face poked through the hole, beckoning us inside.

One after another, we managed to get the forty or so of us into the cave as we realized where we were: a fourth-century

---

50 Turkish staff names have all been changed for safety concerns and privacy.

church. We stood in the nave, marveling at the cross-shaped room carved into the rock and the faded, red-frescoed walls. Murat stood in front and withdrew from his bag a red clay goblet, a bottle of wine, and a loaf of bread. As he prepared the sacraments, another Turkish staff woman began to sing a hymn that reverberated in the small space. We were Turkish, American, Korean, Kiwi, Australian, Azeri, Albanian, and British. Turkish was our common language, which is to say much was left unsaid. He led us in communion while the Koreans led us in prayer, and Ela kept singing, and we all knew we were on holy ground.

Crowded into this ancient holy place, hidden along the path in a valley untouched by tourists, we were united by a simplified version of our faith. When language ability failed us, the shared love of Jesus was all we had left. At that moment, it felt like enough. How long did we linger in that sacred space? Surely our four-year-old did not patiently wait around. In my memory, we soak in the sun's rays shining through a crack in the ceiling. We listen to Ela sing until her voice fades. We pray all at once, as the Koreans pray, until we have no more words to speak. And we exit from the hole in the valley wall in silence, aware of how close we were to heaven.

In those days, my focus would have been on finding hints of a church long swallowed up by Islam. In my Istanbul neighborhood, I walked by Greek and Armenian churches, which were emptied of parishioners since the infamous population exchange of the 1920s, but still stood and were open for the curious Turk to enter and light candles.[51] I looked for crosses the

---

51 In 1923, following the Greco-Turkish War, in an effort to bring stability and prevent further conflict, 1.5 million people in Turkey and Greece were forced to relocate/swap homelands as part of the Treaty of Lausanne.

way my preschooler looked for trucks. In a skyline dominated by the minarets of mosques, a cross atop a steeple was both rare and historic. But back then, my curiosity did not extend to the people who built the churches. I would have never considered the fingerprints of women left behind. I just did not know. I had not yet been awakened to the feminine story.

As we retraced our steps back through the valley that day, I had no idea I was walking in the footsteps of great saints, church fathers and mothers, contributors to the Nicene Creed, and some of the last female voices before the great silencing brought forth by church council after church council.

Today, as I sip my third cup of coffee, my thoughts return to that holy day in the cave church and I wonder who commissioned it, whose figure is outlined behind the altar, who gathered to worship in secret, and who led the service. If I were to find the church again, would I find evidence of the woman I imagine left her fingerprints? And could it be one of the Cappadocian mothers? One of the great lineages of women I've been tracing? Could I have been in one of their churches and not known it?

By the third century, the gospel had saturated Asia Minor in what is now modern Turkey. The Roman Empire was ruled by a triumvirate that took turns persecuting Christians. The worst of the worst was Diocletian, whose palace was located in what is today Split, Croatia. From his seat of power, he ruled the Eastern empire and decreed such violence against the followers of Jesus that it is estimated some 3,500 were martyred.

Enter the Cappadocian power couple of the fourth century: Emmelia and Basil the Elder. These two were raised by families of strong believers who suffered under Diocletian.

Emmelia was the daughter of wealthy martyrs, and Basil was the son of Macrina the Elder, who went into hiding during the persecutions.

As you might imagine, the stone of the valley must have been quite soft if people could carve out a church from inside a cave with the rudimentary tools of the fourth and fifth centuries. Indeed, the Cappadocian landscape was formed from the lava of the Mount Erciyes volcano, and throughout the centuries, inhabitants carved out shelter both above and below ground. Entire cities crisscross this underground region, up to eighteen stories deep in the ones excavated. Today, visitors duck through narrow tunnels to explore the honeycomb hiding places of early Christians. Churches with altars are prominent in each underground city, along with large round stone barriers strategically placed to quickly roll into place to seal off the floor below from attack.

By the time Emmelia was married, she and Basil enjoyed the relative religious peace of the fourth century. Basil was a wealthy rhetorician, and they were parents to nine children, five of whom became Orthodox Saints.[52] This would be enough to appreciate the legacy established in these two generations, but the story gets better.

Their oldest daughter, Macrina the Younger, was engaged to be married at age twelve, but after her fiancé died, she declared she would remain a virgin all her days to serve the Lord. When her father died ten or fifteen years later, Macrina and her mother, Emmelia, retreated to family property and began a monastic community.

---

52 The five who became saints were the following: Macrina the Younger, Basil the Great, Gregory of Nyssa, Peter of Sebaste, and Naucratius.

Monasticism was spreading among Christians who believed the best way of becoming like God was through celibacy and dedication to prayer, study, and a quiet life of service. The women started health centers, soup kitchens, and related services in the community while living equitably with one another. Radically, Macrina freed her slaves and lived out Paul's proclamation—there is no longer slave nor free, male nor female. Supposedly, after studying in Athens, her brothers Gregory of Nyssa and Basil the Great returned home, rather pompous with all their knowledge. She is said to have put Basil in his place, after which he repented and entered the monastic life as well.

Gregory and Basil went on to become famous bishops and were present for the Second Ecumenical Council of Constantinople, called in 381 CE by the Emperor to reaffirm what had been decided at the Council of Nicea in 325 CE. It's difficult to understand the nature of the seven official church councils that convened between 325 and 787 CE— the degree to which fighting, banishment, spying, and even murder occurred, and how orthodoxy gradually evolved. The creeds we recite now (and probably take for granted) were hard fought.

While the men were duking out the nature of Christ, the women were leading the spiritual life of their communities. Some were referred to as deaconesses, the highest rank given to women in that era.[53] They cared for the sick, ministered to the needy, served communion, baptized fellow women, and even

---

53 Women served as deacons from the beginning of the Church. "I commend to you our sister Phoebe, a deacon of the church in Cenchreae." Romans 16:1, NIV.

carried letters to other cities. The Cappadocians believed that the role of women in the life of the church on earth was evidence of how things were and would be in heaven (meaning, non-gendered). And while they may have been excluded from priestly and bishopric duties on earth, it would not be like that in heaven. Which is to say, it ought not to have been like that, and they knew it.

Women were so present in leadership in the early church that the 451 CE Council of Chalcedon included requirements for the ordination of deaconesses, and the Apostolic Constitutions (which were essentially manuals for clergy) contained an ordination prayer for deaconesses:

> *O Eternal God, the Father of our Lord Jesus Christ, the Creator of man and of woman, who didst replenish with the Spirit Miriam, and Deborah, and Anna, and Huldah; who didst not disdain that Thy only begotten Son should be born of a woman; who also in the tabernacle of the testimony, and in the temple, didst ordain women to be keepers of Thy holy gates, —do Thou now also look down upon this Thy servant, who is to be ordained to the office of a deaconess, and grant her Thy Holy Spirit, and "cleanse her from all filthiness of flesh and spirit," that she may worthily discharge the work which is committed to her to Thy glory, and the praise of Thy Christ, with whom glory and adoration be to Thee and the Holy Spirit for ever. Amen.[54]*

---

54 *Apostolic Constitutions*, "Book VIII, No. 20," in *Apostolic Constitutions*, WomenPriests.org, https://womenpriests.org/tradition/ aposcon2-the-apostolic-constitutions-book-viii/#deaconess.

Macrina led her community for years and passed on leadership to her sister (or sister-in-law; it's unclear), Theosebia, the Deaconess of Nyssa. On her deathbed, Macrina's brother Gregory came to tend to her, and at her passing, he and her closest female attendant, Vetiana, divided the necklace she wore around her neck. Vetiana took the cross while Gregory took a little ring that encased a hollow stone with a fragment of *the* cross. We know all of the details of Macrina's death because her brother wrote about it in *The Life of Saint Macrina*, but we do not know where she obtained the cross fragment.

Could it have been from Helena, Constantine's mother, a believer long before her son claimed the faith, who visited the Holy Land and is the one who commissioned the churches that still stand in Bethlehem and Jerusalem? Her image is in all of the small cave churches in Cappadocia, as she was a revered Saint from the beginning. Legend has it that she went in search of the true cross and is believed to have found it. To test whether it was real or not, she held a piece of the wood above a dead body, and it came to life. Did Helena find *the* cross and bring it back through Cappadocia on her way home to Constantinople? And, even if it wasn't the actual cross, did fourth-century Christians believe it to be? Macrina may have.

Not too far away, Macrina's brothers' close friend, Gregory of Nazianzus, was raised by a pious woman named Nonna. She was a believer long before her husband and prayed for him until he came to faith. Eventually, he became a bishop, and she a deaconess, and their children became leaders in the church. Their daughter, Gorgonia the Righteous, as she was known, raised five children, two of whom also became bishops. Another incredible legacy of the faith, a picture of strong and faithful women raising strong and faithful children.

Unfortunately, due to their commitment to virginity, monastic communities did not continue to produce children, and by the close of the fourth century, the Cappadocian influence began to wane. The fingerprints of Macrina the Elder, Emmelia, Macrina the Younger, Theosebia, Nonna, Gorgonia, and other female leaders of the region would become so faint that the thick museum textbook detailing every cave church would make no mention of them, nor would a present-day tour guide have ever heard of them. Despite the number of times I had visited their homeland, I had never heard of them, either. Experts, historians, guides, and residents knew nothing of the women who had literally shaped the landscape. It was not until years later that I would slowly discover their fingerprints.

When did the women begin to disappear? Did it start with the rise of Augustine in the late fourth century, the Bishop of Hippo and arguably the most influential voice since Paul? Some say his low opinion of women merely reflected the times, while others argue his misogynistic views negatively impacted the role of women in the church and how the women who shaped the church were remembered (or not). Was it after the Council of Chalcedon in 451 CE, to which over 520 male bishops attended? As church hierarchy became codified, and with the release of the "Apostolic Constitutions," did it become more important in a patriarchal society to officially suppress the female voice?

Here is what we know: The women of the New Testament—those who funded and hosted the early church, carried Paul's letters and discipled new believers, the martyrs who refused to recant their faith during severe Roman persecution, the Cappadocian and Egyptian Desert Mothers who chose a life of chastity to know God better, the deaconesses who baptized and served communion and were ordained in the church—led in the first few centuries in ways we have not seen since. Where they went and for what reason they became increasingly invisible is not within the scope of this book, but it haunts me.

It's why I'll linger in the cave churches of Cappadocia until I've noted each and every female figure in the painted walls. It's why I'll labor to copy the Greek letters of a questionable figure, and upon learning the name is female, spend the time researching Barbara and Catherine and Eudocia and Salome and Mia and Theodota. Who were these sisters of mine whom history forgot; the ones who went before me in this land and left their mark, not only on these cities I love, but on my faith and in my church and for my daughters; the great cloud of witnesses who joined us on that holy day while Ela sang and Murat blessed the sacraments and the Koreans prayed?

The pilgrimage group is with me in a cave church off the beaten path, stewarded by the farmer whose land it is on. So much damage has been done to the frescoed faces that we can barely make out any of them. Are those wishes scratched in Greek next to the year 1895? The interior is in the shape of a square cross, with a small altar in the apse. On this second pilgrimage, there's a singer among us, and she stands in the apse where the natural acoustics carry her angelic voice. Later, she will do the same in the amphitheater in Ephesus. Her song morphs into the doxology, and we are surprised to hear the deep bass of our tour guide join the refrain.

I have not yet shared about Emmelia, Macrina, and Theosebia with this group, and decide this perhaps is the best place to do so. The women urge me to stand at the altar where

my voice carries, and it does not escape any of us: I am preaching to women, about women, in an ancient church in a land in
which women used to do the same shamelessly.

My stories bring them to life, but as I look at the defaced
figures painted on the ceilings and walls around us, I realize that
in sainthood, their humanity was erased. Perhaps it was the only
way to memorialize significant women. Still, in the same way
I've elevated their contribution and ignored the complexity of
their choices, hagiography (the inflated biography of a saint)
idealizes rather than humanizes these sisters. In doing so, we
rob them of their embodied selves. We make them *other* and
therefore perpetuate the enormity of the distance between our
reality and those we would emulate.

What if we received the vandalism as a gift? A reminder
that long before they were saints, they were women in the flesh
who made complicated choices that yielded incredible fruit
and unforeseen consequences. This particular church invited
us to remember their humanity in the same way I believe my
preaching invited them home. Surrounded by a great cloud of
witnesses, bearing testimony to what will be true in heaven even
if it's less than a reality here and now, I preached on.

Do you have a story of your leadership in the church? What is
that story, and how has it shaped you?

PATLICAN SALATISI

Eggplant salad is a classic Turkish meze. While this country isn't the top consumer of eggplant in the world (China is), Turkey is a close second! Eggplant is a featured vegetable in numerous dishes. This meze is served cold, among others such as fava (or butter) beans, yogurt with cucumber, carrot salad, and tons of bread. Prepare a meze table and pretend you're in the cave with us! This one is relatively easy, so long as eggplants are in season:

1. Roast 2 eggplants, about 5 seeded red peppers, and 1 pint of cherry tomatoes at 400 degrees for about 25 minutes. Remove and dice into small chunks.

2. Add 2 pressed garlic cloves, 1 teaspoon lemon, and 1 teaspoon white vinegar.

3. Season with salt to taste. Serve cold.

CERAMICS

YEARS AGO, AN acquaintance asked me to go to coffee and gave me three things: First, though barely knowing one another, we had such an authentic and meaningful conversation that I left wanting more. Second, she wanted to express gratitude (a rare gift indeed) for the work my husband and I did in the community. Third, she wanted to show her appreciation and brought me two of her own handmade ceramic wine glasses. Well, I'm not daft. I asked her to coffee again a few months later, and then again. Over the years, as Rachel and I have developed our friendship, I have simultaneously watched her develop a pottery business, turning those wine goblets into works of art, and eventually, her own studio. Her skill is impressive, but her passion is contagious. When she said yes to coming to Turkey, I knew Avanos would be her highlight.

Nestled along the river, Avanos is a charming town in the Cappadocia region, home to artisans who strive to keep ancient handicrafts alive, and it remains largely unspoiled by tourism. Our tour guide takes us to the oldest family business in the area for a demonstration, where I knew Rachel would have a chance to throw clay. Our group is offered homemade wine and apple tea while we watch a master potter form the famous Hittite wine decanter, a perfectly hollow circle connected to a long stem.[55] The host explains the process, the history of the shape, and so forth, but we're all really waiting for Rachel to take a turn at the wheel.

When the offer is made, she puts on protective pants, and the master positions himself to work the foot wheel, assuming she's just another novice tourist. No, she knows how to throw and work the wheel, *thank you very much*. She starts with a look of barely contained glee as she kicks the wheel and gets the clay thoroughly wet in her hands. The host is already impressed as he realizes she is no beginner. The challenge is not just to form a simple shape, but to replicate the highly complex Hittite decanter. To do so requires her to perfectly fold the top rim over her hands and into itself, creating a hollow circle. For a moment, the clay wobbles, and the host expresses a relieved sigh. Rachel's look turns from glee to determination, still smiling but with absolute resolve. Within seconds, the clay rights in her hands, and she successfully forms the hollowed circle. We cheer as she detaches it from the wheel and shoots her arms into the air in triumph. Our hosts are duly awed. They've never had a fellow master in their shop, let alone a woman!

They lead us into the next room to explain the rest of the process, where four women are sitting at small tables painting intricate designs on plates. We are told the men throw clay and form the pieces, but after the first kiln fire, the women take over, spending hours hand-painting flowers, geometric shapes, or little people for the Hittite replicas. (Elsewhere, we are told

---

55 The Hittite Empire of central Anatolia (Turkey) was a Bronze-age civilization that reached its peak in the mid-14th century BCE.

another story… that women are involved in every step of the process. Turks are nothing but confident in their contradictory explanations.) The women are focused and careful as we watch over their shoulders and slowly make our way to the gallery where samples of the very best pieces are showcased. Rachel has brought one of her own pieces to give to the host, and he returns the honor by giving her one of his. I think she floats out of the shop.

When we returned to Turkey as a family for the first time since leaving, we spent a week in Cappadocia. The girls had never been, and we wanted to vacation in an area of the country we loved. The day we meandered through the windy, cobblestone streets of Avanos turned out to be a formative parenting experience for me.

Far from the tourist stops in the more polished art studios, we walked past tiny shops and singular artisans. In front of one door, we chatted with an older man who was smoking and drinking tea. Putting both his cigarette and tulip glass down, he beckoned us into his little front room, just large enough for three little footstools and his potter's wheel. Hanging from every square inch of the surrounding wall and ceiling was pottery. He demonstrated throwing clay and formed a teapot, all while excitedly talking to my husband in Turkish. (Turkish men won't talk to me if he's around!)

The potter explained that the river, which runs through town, produces red clay that makes Avanos ceramics famous, and he gave us plenty of unpainted gifts to remind us. It's the longest river flowing entirely within Turkey, and it is in Avanos that it deposits red clay. From my Christmas tree hang five small pots, on our bookshelf we display a pitcher, and countless people have shared communion from the goblet my husband takes to retreats. The river flows far from our doorstep but courses through the veins of our lives.

The kids each took a turn at the wheel and had a good laugh, especially when my son lost control and clay flew into his face. Then, it was time to shop. We had not noticed the darkened descent into the cave behind us until the artisan turned on the lights. A few small steps led into a long room lined with stacks of plates, bowls, trivets, and decanters. We had either seen most of the samples in the Grand Bazaar in Istanbul or already owned similar ones, but there was one style we had not seen: blue, lace-like votives. The artisan noticed our interest and put one in my hand before turning the lights off and sending the room into absolute darkness. The next thing I knew, he lit the candle and pointed to the ceiling, where the delicate carvings in the votive cast a beautiful pattern of light.

This dear man unknowingly offered me a perspective shift on parenting that I've shared with hundreds of parents since. At the wheel, as I watched him mold the teapot in his hands, I realized how often I had been told to mold and shape, teach and train my children the way a potter works with clay. Yet, how often it felt futile, especially when they were younger! When he took us into the darkened cave and showed us the kaleidoscope of light, I wondered if God actually already had a fully formed masterpiece in my children and wanted me to discover their glory through it. Maybe my role was not to play Potter, but to point my kids to how they reflect the one in whose image they were made.

We left Avanos with five blue votives and a whole new vision of parenting, but it would be another four years before I would search for the role women played in this magnificent region.

❧

Like most towns and cities in Anatolia, Avanos goes back millennia. Hittite references to the city from the second millennium BCE and pottery shards that date to the early Bronze Age have been found here. When Hellenization spread east toward India, Avanos was called *Venessa*, and after the rise of the Roman empire, *Ouenasa*. Interestingly, in the local dialect of Phrygian Greek, *Ouenasa* meant queen and *Venasa* meant goddess. It is thought that the city worshiped Cybele, the universal creator and mother of all gods.[56] Cybele was first and foremost an Anatolian goddess dating from at least 600 BCE, but she was later incorporated into Greek and Roman mythology and eventually morphed into "Magna Mater," mother god of Rome. Some scholars believe the worship of Artemis in Ephesus was conflated with Cybele, leading us into the second century CE.

In the Museum of Anatolian Civilizations in the capital city of Ankara, visitors can see the transformation of the mother goddess throughout time as represented in statues found around the region. Starting with the oldest civilization is the sixth-millennium BCE statue of a seated woman with voluptuous breasts, flanked by felines. From there, we see the thirteenth-century BCE Hittite goddess, Kubaba (also seated with a feline at her feet). In the ninth century BCE, we see the Phrygian goddess, Kybele, and in the fourth century BCE, we see the early Greek goddess Cybele, sitting flanked by felines. At the turn of the millennium, we see the second-century CE Roman Mater, sitting flanked by felines.

---

56 "Avanos," *Turkish Archaeological News*, submitted December 21, 2016, last modified January 10, 2017, https://turkisharchaeonews. net/content/avanos.

Archaeologists found the 8,000-year old figurine of the voluptuous woman, clearly mid-birth, and flanked by felines just a three-hour drive south of Avanos, in the oldest known civilization of Çatalhöyük. Imagine. That means the figure was made 3,500 years before the pyramids were built. What does it say that the earliest civilizations worshipped a goddess?

After a quick review, I'm reminded of what I learned in middle school: The Stone Age came first, *then* the Bronze Age, *then* the Iron Age, and *then* written, recorded history. Eight thousand years ago, we were in the Neolithic Age, and people were just beginning to cultivate crops. The Abrahamic Covenant dates back approximately 4,000 years. Now, I don't think we know definitively how many years before Abraham were Noah, Eden, or the dawn of humans. But let's just say there were 4,000 years. Let's say that four millennia *before* God made a covenant with Abraham, humans understood the divine to be feminine. They worshiped a mother, one who gives birth, one who creates life.

In a relatively new underground museum in Avanos, small figurines of goddesses dating back 7,000 years are displayed in sand. These are displayed among the thousands of pottery pieces that span the cultures and millennia represented in this region. In light of my new perspective on the sainthood of significant women, it makes me wonder if the Stone and Bronze Age manner of memorializing amazing women was to deify them as goddesses. Like early Christian saints, the veneration of women in prehistoric times might be far more akin to the American Women Quarters™ Program. Was Cybele a way to understand the universal god, or simply the immortalization of one badass woman in history?

The quiet little riverside town of Avanos awakens my curiosity. On the other side of the river from the underground museum is a Cappadocian "way of life" center where you can learn how to counter the effect of an evil eye or appropriately wield your luck on a wishing tree. And, just a few blocks away is another unusual find: the Hair Museum. Truly the most surprising thing I've ever seen in Turkey, this little room tucked into a cave displays thousands of locks of hair from women all over the world. The family-owned pottery studio says it randomly chooses one lock each year for an all-expense-paid trip and a private lesson from the master potter himself. You better believe I cut a lock from my own head and strategically taped it to the wall.

Unsure if it's the domesticity of the place or the layers and layers of history we walk upon, teeming with figurines of goddesses, but I feel my femininity is a gift in Avanos. In larger cities like Istanbul, both as a foreigner and as a woman, there are times when I want to hide beneath the black chadors of the female Persian Gulf tourists. But in this little town on the edge of the Red River, I feel welcomed, safe.

I admit my study of Cybele and ancient Hittite culture is limited. I know just enough to wonder, as I've done aloud for you here. Would you wonder with me? For if I'm learning anything in my journeys to Turkey, it's that the story of women is not so different from place to place, time to time.

> What do you make of one of the oldest known civilizations worshiping a mother goddess? To what degree have you embraced the mother heart of God?

HITTITE STEW

The Hittites lived in Anatolia during the second millennium BCE, and multiple sites are currently being excavated in modern-day Turkey. The head archaeologist at one of these sites partnered with a chef to recreate recipes translated from cuneiform tablets. Ingredients included beef, olive oil, honey, chickpeas, and grains. In the Cappadocian town of Kayseri, university culinary students are taught these ancient dishes. Here is a recipe for a vegetarian Hittite stew to accompany your discussion on the ancient goddesses of this civilization.[57]

Combine the following ingredients and bring to a boil:

- ½ cup dried, peeled butter beans, soaked overnight (or 1 can, drained)
- ½ cup dried chickpeas, soaked overnight (or 1 can, drained)
- ½ cup lentils
- ½ cup pearl wheat (or pearl spelt, if available)
- ½ cup pearl barley
- 1 tablespoon coriander seeds
- 2 tablespoons butter
- 4 cups vegetable stock

The chef recommends adding sauteed onions, garlic, and spices for more flavor.

---

57 Ursula Janssen, *From Eden to Jerusalem: Recipes from the Time of the Bible* (London: [Independent], 2020).

OYA

WE SETTLE INTO our cave hotel in Cappadocia, and everyone is eager to wander the quieter, fairy tale streets of our town. We are taking a slower pace in Anatolia, the heartland of Turkey, and personalities come out after leaving the stimulation and overwhelm of Istanbul: the shopper, the hiker, the bubble bath taker. I am on the hunt for a particular store.

Four years ago, I met a female entrepreneur in this town who led an artisan co-op. She provided a network of women in the region with jewelry supplies and, from the convenience of home, they produced the beautiful products she sold retail and wholesale around the world. I wanted my current group to meet her and shop in her store, but I knew from Google Maps that the shop was no longer where it had been. Of course, I doubted her business survived the blow to tourism the pandemic caused. I hoped she had found another, smaller option and took off in search of it.

From our hotel, I turned left to wander up the narrow, twisting cobblestone street. Much was familiar, and I fondly remembered the colorful wagon wheels brightening up an otherwise drab, gray stone wall. The last time I had passed, a pink velvet chair rested beneath them. Conveniently, just past this "street art," I found a female artisan shop!

Carved out of the rock, a small shop, no bigger than an American walk-in closet, was full of the handmade traditional jewelry I remembered. In the middle of the room, a circular swing bed was suspended from the ceiling: the traditional baby swing of Turkish villages. A two-year-old boy was following his older sister around the shop, pausing to mind his grandmother, who sat at the little table drinking tea. Opposite her, a young woman shyly looked up at me, continuing to knit beads into the colored thread in her hands. She was not the entrepreneur I met four years ago, but a younger version doing the same handicraft.

I had entered the quintessential female space of central Turkey, where women had been making Oya for thousands of years. Oya, a fine lace knit with various-sized needles and thread, is female art through and through. The scene in the shop—grandmother, daughter, two children running around—was the perfect picture of both the segregation of gender in the Turkish workspace and the industry of women in this land. The only other person missing in this tableau was the neighbor who surely made Oya, too, and helped keep the shop stocked. With their earnings, they could buy school uniforms for their primary-aged children and supplement what their husbands' labor jobs supplied. I know this not from our conversation, but from knowing this land.

When I spoke Turkish, her eyes danced, and the kids started shopping for me, suggesting bracelets, anklets, and chokers. They were delightful. As I kept bumping into the "baby swing," I couldn't help marveling at the beauty of her blurred life. Were we in a business or a home? Was she a stay-at-home mom or a working mom? I didn't want to leave, as most of the outward-facing world of Turkey—the shops, restaurants, and museums—is male. Here I was with the feminine—a peek into the living room "salons" of the Turkish village woman. Where kids played, older aunts and grandmothers doled out advice while drinking tea, and the middle generation managed it all. In Istanbul, women her age were mostly working long hours in demanding jobs (teachers, bank tellers, corporate) and small children were in day care or with a nanny. Ambition and modern expectations catapulted Turkish women into post-secondary education and careers, perhaps an urban-rural dichotomy in much of the world, but one we tend to polarize. One is not necessarily better; not as I enjoy the peace in this little shop, mesmerized by her fingers weaving beads onto thread that is shaping into an intricate lace flower.

Eventually, some of our group wanders into her shop. The kids get to work with their recommendations, and I break the reverie.

I first encountered the art of Oya in the strangest of ways. We were living in Seattle to pursue graduate school, but also to regroup after a hard decade of full-time ministry in Turkey. I still wasn't sure which had bruised me most—the ministry, the place, or God—but grad school was bringing me back to life. I was rediscovering parts of myself that I had put to sleep to survive as a young American mom in Istanbul. I was getting reacquainted with my own heart and recognizing my intuition. For my degree in International Community Development, I was exploring ideas that would lead me back to this country to partner with a different type of work than I had been a part of before.

This was 2009. At the time, the most widely known U.S.-based social enterprise for international artisans was Ten Thousand Villages. The term "cottage industry" had just become trendy, and the idea of buying directly from cooperatives to sell out of homes, churches, and boutiques in the West went hand in hand with the increasing popularity of microlending. The book *When Helping Hurts* was released that same year, and Christians were starting to reevaluate the way they had done missions and humanitarian aid.

I had a friend in Turkey who envisioned fusing ministry and economic development and invited me to consult with a Turkish believer whose recent conversion story was well-known and isolating. She suffered violence from her husband until Jesus appeared to him in a dream. Then they both experienced rejection and shunning from their village when they decided to follow Jesus publicly. But she and my friend shared a goal: He would give her a small loan from which she would buy supplies for Oya, and, working with other women in her village, she would send the finished products to sell in the States. Oya would allow her to work with neighbors and rebuild trust that could lead to faith conversations down the road.

This is why I found myself at three a.m. at a twenty-four-hour rest stop in the middle of nowhere, stumbling down the bus steps and over to the toilets. My body was stiff and confused. It was hard to remember what time zone I was in as I'd been traveling nonstop for two days. I started in Seattle and went to Houston first, then took a fifteen-hour flight to Dubai because a friend had given me points to fly Emirates. I wandered around the airport in my orange juice-stained comfortable outfit, feeling foolishly underdressed among the Arab women. Their shoes and eye makeup were enough proof of the high fashion beneath the black chadors. I then backtracked to Istanbul and transferred to the domestic terminal to zigzag back to Ankara. A Turkish friend picked me up at the airport, gave me a cell phone, and drove me to the bus terminal, where I boarded an overnight bus headed to the village. Presumably, at around 5:30 a.m., we would pull into another twenty-four-hour bus stop, where my friend with the loan would be waiting to drive me to the home of the villager I'd come to meet. While squatting on the Turkish toilet, the first of many doubts washed over me. Why had I left my three, six, and nine-year-olds in Seattle to pee in the middle of nowhere, Turkey, in the middle of the night?

Predictably, the bus stopped at the right place and my friend was waiting for me. It was still dark when we arrived at the village house, and so I didn't see the sheep in the front yard until I had to walk through hundreds of them to get to the outhouse later that morning. The couple prepared a bedroll for me in the small main room, in which seven of us squeezed later when curious neighbors stopped by to meet the foreigners. I slept for an hour or so and woke first to the Call to Prayer and then to bleating sheep. Soon after, our host brought in a basket of fresh bread and a tray with fresh cheese, fruit, and a two-liter of Fanta.

We spent the day walking through the village, stopping at homes, and chatting with some of the women who had agreed to make Oya. None was alone. In one house, a group of women was outside on blankets harvesting a bitter green. In another, they were knitting. I pictured our host sitting with these women, making beautiful jewelry together, and slowly sharing about the man in the dream that changed her life.

∽

Oya has been a language in and of itself for thousands of years. It is thought to have originated in this region in the eighth century BCE by the Anatolian Phrygians.[58] It carries all sorts of meaning and is said to be the most difficult needlework in the world. In Europe, it is known as Turkish Lace. In Anatolia, it is an essential skill for girls to learn. Among women, it is a secret language. The bride gifts handmade Oya to her future mother-in-law, and the colors and flowers she uses signify the degree of her affection for both her future spouse and his parents! Throughout Turkey, the motifs, needles, and thread vary, and the most exquisite silk designs made with sewing needles originally came from the harem of the Ottoman palace.

The thing that remains the same across generations, status, and materials used, is that Oya is made *by, with,* and *for* women. I tried to think of one thing my generation still does that compares. Maybe twenty years ago, it was scrapbooking? Perhaps some women still quilt together. I found myself longing for an ancient handicraft that all of my friends equally knew how to make. Maybe that's one of the reasons companies like Noonday have flourished? What we can't do, we can at least appreciate. A beautiful role reversal for Western women: to depend on our global sisters to make beautiful things for us.

My encounter with the villager who loved both Jesus and her community aroused in me a longing that has yet to be satiated. I would feel it again with the young artisan in Cappadocia,

---

58 Anatolia is Central Turkey, known as the heartland of Turkey, and sits upon layers of history. The Phrygian civilization rose after the collapse of the Hittites, 1200-700 BCE.

knowing she made the bulk of her products alongside friends and neighbors. I would feel it again when taking a class in Rachel's studio, barely talking to the other students sitting elbow to elbow at our wheels. I would feel it in my office, disconnected and disappointed despite my efforts. And I would feel it in the church we finally leave. A local rootedness and communal way of living do not exist in my world.

My thoughts return to the harem of the Ottoman Palace. With the finest silk thread and the tiniest of sewing needles, the harem women must have created the most elaborately decorated scarves, dresses, and robes. Despite the parroted narrative I always hear from guides of how fortunate the concubine slave girls were and how they were treated to an education, lavish accommodation, and the chance to become the mother of the sultan, one thing is undeniable: The women learned the skilled art of Turkish Lace. So well-known was the Ottoman style of beaded embroidery that it is said Catherine de Medici of France brought Ottoman girls to her palace for this purpose.

When I left Turkey in 2007, a friend gifted me a framed piece of nineteenth-century Ottoman embroidery. It looks like lace tulips on muslin. I wonder who wove those tiny red beads into such delicate flower shapes. Was she in the harem? Did she sit on a carpet or against a pillow in a room full of other concubines? Was there laughter or embittered gossip? What did they do with their trauma? How did it live in their bodies and infuse daily life in the harem? Did the rhythmic and somatic art of Oya soothe their heartache or quell their fear? Did they become a sisterhood, more united than competitive or jealous?

When I consider the various groups of girls or women with

whom I've experienced the most intimate connection, I recall far more both/and than either/or. We were supportive *and* jealous. We celebrated *and* grieved, had fun *and* were serious. I imagine the harem was like that. And I imagine the village women and the Cappadocian artisans are similar. I can long for what they have and recognize it for what it is: a simplicity of life and a form of communal living fast becoming rare. I have a nostalgia for something I've never known, yet my soul knows. Is that sort of nostalgia a taste of heaven? A little window into how things will be in eternity? A small reminder of where we are, actually, citizens? For now, I will sit with the longing and ponder how we American women might develop a secret language of our own.

> Do you know a space with the women of your life that mirrors Oya making? If not, do you long for it? What do you do with that longing? What could you do with it?

SIGARA BÖREĞI

When you go to tea at a friend's home in Turkey, she will bring out a platter of various foods that will definitely include some sort of börek. Using thinly rolled sheets of dough called yufka (or phyllo dough), she layers chopped greens, feta, and parsley. Sometimes she boils it, sometimes she fries it. My favorite version is the rolled and fried kind that is literally called cigarette börek. This is easy to make and becomes a classic afternoon snack to share with friends as you wonder together about the spaces women inhabit.

1. You'll need phyllo dough, feta, parsley, an egg, some salt, and oil for frying.

2. Mix a container of feta, chopped parsley, one beaten egg, and some salt.

3. Make sure you are working with fresh, damp phyllo (keeping covered what you aren't working with). Unwrap one sheet at a time. Fold in half. Place 2 tablespoons of the feta mix into the middle. Roll like a cigarette and set aside (again, covered) on a plate. When you're finished rolling all of them, refrigerate while your oil gets hot.

4. Fry until golden brown and drain on a paper towel. Eat hot.

NARGILE

I CONSTRUCTED A tight and tidy faith to carry me through my teens. It may have been the road less traveled in my high school, but I found it to be an easier path on Friday nights when decisions were made. It meant I graduated from high school and college with a very clean slate, which worked well for the mission's application, ironically landing us in a country with one of the highest percentages of smokers in the world (33% of the population).

That first year in Turkey, my husband and I reeked of smoke from spending day after day in student canteens, inhaling the toxic fumes of cheap cigarettes for the sake of the gospel. It was 1997, and Turks did not seem to be aware of the health risks associated with secondhand smoke. They smoked on ferries, in taxis, in restaurants. When Starbucks opened in 2003, it was the first public place we had ever been in Turkey that was smoke-free. (It wouldn't be until 2009 that the government banned smoking inside public spaces, and even now it's marginally enforced.)

During our first summer there, we welcomed a team of American college students and staff leaders for six weeks. They helped with campus outreach and infused life, energy, and deep conversation into our little team. We were all living a tight and tidy faith, and we spent hours discussing the boxes, walls, and frameworks we were protecting.[59] Imagine my surprise, then, when during the last retreat, one of the American leaders pulled out a pack of cigarettes and challenged the women to take a drag. Were she not my favorite, not my senior, I never would have dared. Good girls don't smoke. And we certainly don't break rules. And Beth doesn't like to get in trouble. But I did it. I took my turn and inhaled, coughed, and laughed as Jill invited us all to lighten up.

As the years went by, Turkish students kept smoking cigarettes, but something else grew in popularity: the nargile. Known in America by its original Persian name, *hookah*, the water pipe made its way to the Ottoman Empire in the seventeenth century and became a status symbol. Apparently, if you smoked with the sultan, you were someone important indeed.

I remember first encountering these exotic water pipes on a trip to Cairo. We had to leave Turkey every three months for a new tourist visa and looked for the cheapest flights to new destinations. The Temple of Hatshepsut had been bombed in November 1997, and by February 1998, prices bottomed out in Egypt. We took a Nile Cruise for a few hundred dollars! So young and naive, the "tour guide" we paid to take us to the pyramids smuggled us in on camelback through a hole in the fence and then abandoned us while we were inside the first pyramid. Later that night, desperate for a reprieve, we went to an Italian restaurant in the main square, and I remember walking through

---

59 A lot of us vs. them thinking and black and white beliefs about doctrine, salvation, and sanctification defined this stage of our faith and ministry.

a haze of sweet smoke wafting from the plaza full of tables of men sitting next to tall, ornate hookahs.

As we made our home in Istanbul in the early 2000s, we watched nargile cafes pop up throughout our neighborhood. Young men and women frequented Starbucks during the day and nargile cafes at night, meeting up with friends and talking late into the evening. The nargile also uses tobacco, but the smoke smell is sweet because many of the flavors are fruity. For the chronic user, it is still an unhealthy habit, but an exotic one and classier than a pack of Camels (the most widely used brand in Turkey). The nargile had become quite trendy.

The nargile experience begins by choosing a flavor of tobacco. Apple is popular, as are pomegranate, peach, and cappuccino. The cafe employee sets it up for you and brings out the water pipe with the hot coals on top and clean mouthpieces for all. The group shares the hose, passing it around and inserting their own mouthpieces, inhaling slowly and waxing philosophical. It is the Turkish version of Paris Bohemia in the 1920s.

Though Jill broke through some of my rigid standards, I never smoked a nargile while living in Turkey. It wasn't until my husband took our son back when he was twelve that they purchased one, and now, on occasion, we sit around our Colorado fire pit sharing an apple pipe with our kids.

Midway through one of our pilgrimages, I invite the women to the carpeted terrace of our cave hotel after dinner. Without the big city lights, Göreme is dark and refreshingly cool. I have a surprise. As they arrange themselves on the kilim pillows and adjust their legs around each other, the hotel staff brings two nargile for us to try: peach and strawberry. Even though this group shares a fierce independence, my invitation to smoke feels wild. I am still the girl who does not like to get in trouble, and they have read me well. It is as unexpected from me as it is welcomed. Eyes start to shimmer with anticipation. I have read them well, too.

The hoses are passed around as stories are shared. In between, we marvel at someone's honed and experienced skill as she expertly blows rings of smoke. It is not entirely surprising that she possesses this skill. What is surprising, however, is the last woman to take a turn. She is the one among us who most needs to throw caution to the wind. The one whose tight and tidy world was imposed on her by a controlling parent. Her story has been stirred, and the reach for the hose is measured, weighty. The others are talking as she takes it into her mouth, but I have locked eyes with hers, and they are full of defiance. After she inhales, a mischievous smile alights her face, and then, "If my mother could see me now."

I can't help it. I fall back into the pillow and clap with delight. It is the statement of the night! Oh, the freedom to step away from suffocating expectation; to step away from a ruling narrative into another that is far more life-giving! I know because in my own small way, I did that with Jill and a cigarette twenty-five years ago. Whether we are suppressed by another or by ourselves, all too often we suffer the rigid confines of the boxes in which we find ourselves. When did we agree that that was where we belonged? The nargile invites the wild woman forth. Under the stars of the Cappadocian night sky, another metaphor ushers in someone's transformation.

※

In my travel backpack, I allocate space for two books related to these pilgrimages: a Turkish fiction book and David Benner's

The Gift of Being Yourself. Benner is the perfect companion because he invites me, year after year, to curiosity around my own soul. I ask the same questions of myself as I do of the women, and the very first one is always "What question are you bringing into this trip?" Time after time, only at the end of our pilgrimage, when an answer presents itself, do I realize the question I was actually carrying was different than the one I thought.

The year I wrestle with my own complexity, I describe to the women the dichotomy in how history records notable women. On the one hand, women such as Theodora were scandalously sexualized by threatened and patriarchal historians like Procopius in *Secret History*. On the other hand, women such as Macrina were deified through sainthood. In both scenarios, we are deprived of their humanity. Both defamation and veneration replace everyday struggles with archetypal attributes, making them inaccessible to the rest of us. Complexity is a bleak alternative to the divine. And so history gave us angels and demons.

Benner quotes Thomas Merton, and his words burrow deep within me: "*To be a saint means to be myself.*" They accompany me in the cave as I preach that the sainthood of Macrina took her away from us. And they are there in Ephesus when I get my tattoo, permanently marking Theodora's monogram on my body. The impossibility of being one or the other, angelic or demonic, glorious or depraved, all good or all bad! I don't want to be divine. I had been living as if that was the goal. I needed to be good, to be *believed* as good. Constructing a neat and tidy faith came naturally to my Type A, Enneagram 1, need-to-bring-order-out-of-chaos self and yielded a neat and tidy life. There's much beauty in that, and there's a rigidity that binds me to a lesser version of myself. The previous year, I had encountered multiple fractured relationships without closure that left me shattered. *If I'm not all good, am I okay?* At the altar in the Cappadocian cave, I realized I had been forcing myself into sainthood, demanding miracles and veneration of my own soul. What if I let that version of myself off the pedestal? What if I get to be human? What if that's saintly?

In Cappadocia, we worshiped in caves among the memories of our sainted sisters: Emmelia, Macrina, Nonna, Gorgonia, and so many more. They evidenced the spread of the gospel despite persecution, as did the tunnels and defense mechanisms of the underground cities upon which they lived. Operating in the absence of church order and hierarchy, they functioned as deaconesses while securing control of their own bodies and destiny by choosing virginity. Their legacy is in what we hold orthodox today; they shaped the men who debated the details of the Trinity, the essence of Jesus being fully man and fully god, and the role of Mary. But as virgins, the faith they practiced in the cave churches of Anatolia died with them. As a great curtain fell on the role of women in the church, the monastic women provided no voice of dissent. And with their passing came the era of silencing of the female.

These women who left their mark in the third and fourth centuries fill our imaginations. These women who chose virginity, lived in community, and studied the way of Jesus offer a striking parallel to the women of the harem who were robbed of sexual choice, forced to live among each other, and studied the way of the sultan. As I've said along the way, the further back in history we go, the more authority and spiritual influence women had. The faces immortalized on the frescoed cave walls of the rock-hewn churches we visit are evidence of their piety. How might we find evidence of their humanity?

> *What boxes have you rigidly confined yourself to? How might you throw caution to the wind and rebelliously live a different narrative?*

SÜTLAÇ

A nargile is often served with a platter of fresh and dried fruits and nuts or plates of sweets such as lokum and baklava. As a nod to this pairing (with or without the nargile), I invite you to make the Turkish version of rice pudding. If you're like me, you aren't excited about pudding at all, especially one with rice in it. However, sütlaç is truly marvelous![60] Easy and inexpensive to make, serve this in individual ramekin dishes alongside apple tea. Throw caution to the wind!

1. Place 1 tablespoon of rice and ⅔ cup of water in a pan and cook over medium heat, stirring often, until all of the water is absorbed.
2. Place 4 cups of milk in a pan and add rice and a pinch of salt. Bring to a boil.
3. In the meantime, in a bowl, mix 1 tablespoon of cornstarch, ½ tablespoon of rice flour, and ½ cup of cold water until smooth. Gradually add to the boiling milk, stirring constantly for about 10 minutes.
4. Add ½ cup of sugar and continue stirring for 20 minutes, or until the mixture is thickened.
5. Pour into six ramekin dishes and refrigerate for 2-3 hours.
6. Before serving, let it sit at room temperature for an hour. Sprinkle with cinnamon.

---

60 Neşet Eren, *The Art of Turkish Cooking* (Istanbul: [Publisher], 1993).

PART 4

EPHESUS: WALKING IN FREEDOM

1ST CENTURY

IF WE HAVE listened to our soul and noticed where we have been poked and provoked, delighted and invited, stretched and challenged, we enter our last leg of the journey ready to receive God's unique care. The women of the desert have stirred us. The themes we have named in their lives take up residence in ours. Where detailed history is absent, the shared story of the feminine soul fills in the gaps. We know what was true for them because we know what is true for us. And yet, they could not have known how their choices would impact us.

While the congestion of Istanbul unmasked us and the sensual (hamam) and sexual (harem) evoked some of the most intimate parts of our femininity, the monasticism of Cappadocia has left us on the precipice of change. These fourth-century women, either out of pure piety or in equal measure fear of bodily risk, chose a virginal life that they might serve, worship, and become more like God. On the cusp of the church sunsetting women's leadership in ministry, their choice had consequences. It is no small thing to say that we have suffered as a result. Did they know change was afoot? Did they know how radical a faith they had "enjoyed" and suffered for these last few centuries? Another city, further back in time, and we discover how radical it was.

We have been following ancient paths, traversing timelines as we make our way to the sea and the most ancient road yet. Our journey has led us backward in time to a city of women. Known for the Virgin Mary's resting place, the Greek goddess Artemis' temple, and the lore of being founded by the Amazons, you know it as Ephesus. And it is to Ephesus we must go for the final unveiling of Jesus' revolutionary view of women. For it is here that we will rewrite the narrative that women were written out of. At the sea, we will walk in a path of freedom.

AGORA

EPHESUS USED TO be a port city on the Aegean Sea, and at its height of importance, it was the fourth largest city in the ancient world (Rome, Alexandria, and Antioch surpassed it). Today, the bay is silted in, and the entrance to the city sits about 3.5 miles from the water. She was first a Greek city and acquired all of the cultural and linguistic heritage of the Greeks. We have Alexander the Great to "thank" for the Hellenization of the known world in the fourth century BCE. "Thanks" to his endless push East, establishing Greek civilizations upon local ones, the theater became the central dispersion of cultural, political, and economic discourse, and Greek became what English is to the world today.

When the Romans conquered Greece, they modernized cities by introducing plumbing, bathhouses, and improving existing roadways (built mainly by the Persians) with flood protection and sewage systems. Over time, the Romans "paved" some 50,000 miles of roads. By the time Paul and the disciples began their missionary journeys, the Greeks had made it possible to communicate the gospel more widely, and the Romans had made it more accessible.

The Roman road in Ephesus is our first stop as we enter the city from the opposite end of the old port. It's hard to convey my awe of a road, something I would never dream of pointing out to any visitor to my hometown today. The marble slabs are enormous, maybe three feet by five feet. And the length of what is still completely intact is astounding. I am at a loss for words to describe this. To think that what is visible to us is just a small percentage of what exists all the way east to Iran and west to England, beneath layers of earth and subsequent civilizations!

We have just entered the ancient city of Ephesus, and the words of Jeremiah echo: "Go stand at the crossroads and look around." What will we do with the ancient wisdom of the women we have met thus far on our journey, and who are we about to meet?

We all carry stories. It doesn't matter the group of women I'm with, their age range, or their faith background. We all grapple with past experiences that didn't feel quite right, are shedding beliefs that no longer make sense, and are longing for a new narrative around women in the church. Some know dismissal from professors in Bible school, others from pastors and elders, some merely by the air we breathed.[61] To be a Christian female is to wrestle with Paul's words to Timothy, bishop of Ephesus: "I do not permit a woman to teach or to have authority over a man; she is to keep silent. For Adam was formed first, then Eve, and Adam was not deceived, but the woman was deceived

---

61 Meaning the entire atmosphere in which we lived. By osmosis, this is what we absorbed as truth.

and became a transgressor. Yet she will be saved through childbearing, provided they continue in faith and love and holiness, with self-control."[62] Well, great, we'll just shut up and have babies. *What do we do with Paul's words in First Timothy?*

I was fourteen years old when Jesus made sense for the first time. At a youth retreat with friends, Jesus was parsed apart from the grandfatherly Santa-like creator and made real, relational, and relatable. I was drawn to the incarnation, but I also needed the structure and clarity offered by evangelical parachurch ministries. And, because I have always given myself entirely to what I commit to, I became a devoted and dutiful follower. I devoured doctrine and adhered to rules, and eventually raised financial support to join the staff of the organization that would lead me to Turkey.

Eight years after that youth retreat, I was in the car with my new husband, driving to Iowa to celebrate our first anniversary, reading aloud *Recovering Biblical Manhood and Womanhood*. We were complementarians, weren't we? I mean, the same guy who wrote *Systematic Theology*, which we loved, edited this evangelical treatise as well, and clearly thought women should be silent in church. We were supposed to agree, right? But after reading a few essays, we stopped talking about it, neither one of us very convinced.[63]

---

62 1 Timothy 2:12-15, NRSVUE

63 In 1987 the Council of Biblical Manhood and Womanhood issued the Danvers Statement and described complementarianism: a biblical basis for "different but equal." Male headship, female submission, and roles in the church and home were primary. In response, in 1988 the Council of Biblical Equality described egalitarianism: a

A few years later, I would reluctantly use *Five Aspects of Woman* in my college girls' bible study, teaching about feminine roles like "Mistress of the Domain" and "Glory of Man," while trying to suppress my doubt that any of it was actually what Jesus taught. As a college minister, girls often asked about my role in our marriage. There were so many assumptions around *submission* and *spiritual leadership*. I spent most of those early years full of shame that Chris and I were mutually submissive, came to decisions together, and led one another spiritually. What we lived out with each other seemed counter to our entire world. The air I breathed told me something radically different than my gut.

The problem was Paul. I just didn't know what to do with his words.

Paul started to confuse me when I read Romans 16 more closely. Among the list of twenty-nine individuals he addresses, ten are women, and two of these women lead the list: Phoebe, the one who carried the letter, and Priscilla, who co-pastored with her husband Aquila in Rome, Corinth, and later in Ephesus. Of the ten women named, seven are commended for the ministry they performed (compared to only three of the men).[64] The letter to the Romans is believed to have been written by Paul

---

biblical basis for shared leadership between men and women in all spaces.

64 Margaret Mowczko, "A List of the 29 People in Romans 16:1–16," *Marg Mowczko Blog*, May 18, 2019, https://margmowczko.com/list-of-people-in-romans-16_1-16/#:~:text=Twenty%2Dnine%20people%20are%20mentioned.

and sent from Corinth, where he met both Phoebe and Priscilla. Corinth is the city to which he wrote that women should cover their heads and be silent in church, some of his most confusing statements regarding the role of women. The two letters present quite a conundrum. Does Paul affirm or condemn the ministry of women?

And what was I to do with his letter to Timothy? Paul wrote that women should dress modestly, learn and conduct themselves quietly, and would be saved through childbearing! The air I had always breathed used these verses to exclude women from leadership in the church. Years later, my daughter would be told by a pastor she would have to do "mental gymnastics to come to a different conclusion."[65] While 180 women are mentioned as deaconesses, house church leaders, benefactresses, and more in the New Testament, Paul's few verses written to one subset have been used by theologians to diminish them. If Jesus elevated women, was Paul just a misogynist?

What did Timothy do with this letter? As a leader in the city of Ephesus, what was the context for Paul's instructions? Did he share it with the house church leader 123 miles away in Laodicea—a woman named Nympha?[66] Did it get passed to the nearby church in Colossae, led by a woman named Apphia?[67] And what would Timothy's local leaders, Priscilla and Aquila, have thought?

Throughout our years of living in Turkey, we traveled to

---

65 Ella Bruno, oral presentation by guest speaker, Del Ray Baptist Church, Alexandria, VA, at a church-led Bible study, 2022.

66 Colossians 4:15-16

67 Philemon 1:2

Ephesus multiple times. On the other side of the valley is a Christian retreat center where we used to host student weekends, and I remember hiking up the hill once to the ruins rumored to be the prison where Paul was held. We would stand in the amphitheater and talk about the riots Paul caused over disrupting the economy centered on Artemis, and there was always a singer among us who was coaxed into testing the famous acoustics. Paul was the hero of our tours. We never talked about Timothy, Priscilla, or Aquila, and we never even learned about Artemis, the goddess who caused all the uproar.

But it was Artemis who would redeem Paul for me.

Artemis of Ephesus is portrayed in statues with a turban on her head, bee hives at her feet, and various animals on the bottom half of her robe. The turban is a queen symbol, and the animals are a nod to her role as mother of nature and animals. The bees have multiple meanings. Legend has it that the Amazon warriors followed bees to the city they established as Ephesus.[68] Bees were also seen as mythical because they alone could predict the weather. A Queen Bee did not need males to reproduce, an interesting fact in this feminized city. And honey was often used by goddesses in incense for prophecy. But the most recognizable and confusing part of the Artemis statue is the over twelve sacks that hang from her torso. Archaeologists have debated whether these are breasts, for they have no nipples. Some have argued that they are bull testicles. Others say they are beehives.

---

68 Amazonians, female warriors and hunters prominent in Greek mythology and on pottery that fills Turkish museums, make you wonder, myth or no?

The Cult of Artemis was strong in Ephesus. Her temple was one of the seven wonders of the world (today, one lone pillar has been symbolically reconstructed), and the city's economy was dependent on her worshippers. She was the daughter of Zeus and Leto, and the twin sister of Apollo, whom she preceded in birth and then assisted in delivering. Therefore, she was known to protect and assist women in childbirth; to not worship her as a married woman (at risk of conceiving) could quite literally mean death. Her followers showed their devotion by dressing lavishly and wearing expensive jewelry. They walked around aggressively declaring their superiority over men, believing that woman, Artemis, was the author of mankind.

In light of who Artemis was to first-century Ephesians, consider Paul's instructions to Timothy: *Women should adorn themselves modestly, not with braided hair and gold, pearls, or costly attire; women should learn quietly; women should not exercise authority over a man; Adam was formed first and not deceived; she will be saved through childbearing if she continues in faith, love, self-control.*[69] It sounds to me like Paul was speaking directly to the situation in the city to which he was writing. It sounds like what Sandra Glahn explores in *Nobody's Mother*: "How interesting that Paul brings up deliverance through childbirth in a context where false teaching is likely coming from the cult of the goddess of midwifery—especially because he is bringing up a creation story to counter beliefs in a city that prides itself in its goddess's birth."[70]

---

69   1 Timothy 2:9-13, ESV

70   Sandra L. Glahn, *Nobody's Mother: Artemis of the Ephesians in Antiquity and the New Testament* (Downers Grove, IL: InterVarsity Press, 2023), 143.

Paul was a master of using cultural context to teach theological truths. So, what if he was saying something like this: Unlike the cult followers of Artemis, who go around loudly proclaiming superiority over men, dressing in costly clothing, and believing that only she will save them in childbirth, followers of Christ conduct themselves modestly, both in speech and dress, and are submissive to one another. They believe the author of mankind is God; Adam came first, then Eve, who paid the price of sin through painful childbirth and will be saved through faith.[71]

What if Paul wasn't telling women to shut up and have babies, but was actually teaching Ephesian believers about their equality in Christ? In fact, while in Ephesus, Paul wrote to the church in Corinth: "Don't, by the way, read too much into the differences here between men and women. Neither man nor woman can go it alone or claim priority. Man was created first, as a beautiful shining reflection of God—that is true. But the head on a woman's body clearly outshines in beauty the head of her 'head,' her husband. The first woman came from man, true—but ever since then, every man comes from a woman! And since virtually everything comes from God anyway, let's quit going through these "who's first" routines."[72] Or, according to the ESV, "Nevertheless, in the Lord woman is not independent of man nor man of woman." They are equal, just like Jesus showed us.

---

71 Glahn goes into great detail about Paul's use of "saved in childbearing" and what he might have meant. I encourage you to read her work to learn more.

72 1 Corinthians 11:10-12, The Message

While the church in Ephesus expanded, the Cult of Artemis remained. By the fifth century, even though 200 years had passed since the destruction of the Temple of Artemis, the city's cultural identity was still thoroughly infused with her worship. However, deeply rooted in powerful female protectors, the Ephesians' affection for the Virgin Mary, rumored to have come with the Apostle John to spend her last days in the city, had also grown. They had slowly claimed Mary as "theirs," too.

So, when church debates, led by Nestorius, arose that seemingly threatened Mary's importance (naming her Christ-bearer/ Christotokos instead of God-bearer/Theotokos), the city with a long history of the divine feminine may have feared her diminishment. The Ephesians' willingness to supplant Artemis for Mary after the Third Council in 431 CE is striking, shaped as much by theology as culture. It gives me pause to think about these major councils that determined the doctrine we hold to be intractable today. What context informed the decisions?

But that's what happened: Mary replaced Artemis in preeminence. Within a few hundred years, the great city of Ephesus, once among antiquity's top four largest cities, deteriorated due to earthquakes, silting in of the bay, and Arab invasions. Today, Ephesus is just an ancient tourist site, not a modern city, not a zip code. And it's Mary's house and Mary's church that tourists visit, not the great temple. But for those who know, who are familiar with the Cult of Artemis as the backdrop to Paul's words about women, it is a place of true liberation.

As we walk down the Roman road past the library to the agora, the open marketplace where the Artemis trade would have flourished, we imagine her followers, picture their thick, long braids with pearls stuck in every few folds, a gold tiara, and a gold rope holding up their linen robes. They confidently stride into the agora, raising their voice above the cacophony of sellers, declaring, "Great is Artemis, mother of all, creator of all, savior of those in childbirth." They might notice a gathering around a man and pause to listen. What is this blasphemy about women and men being interdependent? About being saved through faith! They sneer and walk on. He's not a threat, yet.

No, he is not a threat. In fact, as we redeem Paul through a feminine and historical reading of scripture, we find healing from our own dismissal. The air we breathe as we exit this ancient city is fresh and clear. We needed every bit of this.

> *Where has Paul been a discouragement in your own life? Where have you known dismissal as a result of these verses? What has the air you have breathed been like? How does hearing of the Cult of Artemis sit with you?*

BAL KAYMAK

AT OUR HOTEL by the sea, the breakfast buffet features a corner section with a massive slab of honeycomb. Guests can cut off a chunk and grab a halved ice cream cone full of clotted cream to eat with it. It's heaven in the morning. In an ancient city whose emblem is a bee, this is the perfect treat to gather around as you discuss Paul. I have found chunks of honeycomb from Turkey and clotted cream from England at World Market!

TERRACES

MY MOTHER-IN-LAW PASSED away recently, and I was in charge of finding photos for the slideshow at her memorial. Providentially, years ago, my father-in-law had all of their old slides converted to digital files. And so it was that I spent a tearful afternoon journeying through her life, from the late forties onward: through the camping vacation her parents took to Arizona, to the year they moved to pre-communist Cuba; the Zuni couple, in their Native dress, holding the blond-haired toddler of their dear friends; all the photos of my mother-in-law in Turkey, starting in the summer of 1963 when she was a high school exchange student, and through the multiple trips she made to visit us forty years later. She loved the place almost as much as I did.

To see Turkey through the years, captured by a foreigner, a tourist, let alone my mother-in-law, was a treasure. She documented over fifty years of small shifts in familiar places: wild, untamed nature surrounding ruins yet to be the archaeological sites I would later visit, the missing sidewalks, scaffolding up, down, and back again in the Hagia Sophia, adding zeros to the Turkish currency, losing zeros, adding zeros again. Time is a slippery thing except when you freeze it in indisputable moments.

When she first came to Ephesus, excavations were just beginning on a portion of the city opposite the Temple of Hadrian, in an area rising into the hillside off the main road. Thirty-five years later, when I first visited, it still wasn't open to the public. In fact, I was finally able to see inside the extraordinary find in 2023.

⌘

I had never paid the extra money to enter the Terrace Homes, but finally I decide it is worth it. I have been researching Roman mosaics, and I've heard they are fully intact in these homes, which we'll walk above on a glass floor. This is where the rich lived. Think brownstones in Manhattan or the white row houses in Mary Poppins' London. The row of townhomes ascends the slope that frames the ancient city. They suspect there are at least six of them, and the Austrians have spent sixty years excavating just two. At some point in the seventh century, they were filled in by landslides and covered in dirt, preserving everything beneath.

As we enter from the Roman road at street level, we immediately see the frescoed walls, mosaic floors, and indoor plumbing of the first century. I am speechless. We ascend the glass staircase to observe the grand hall and fountains, as well as the perfectly intact mosaic floors, save for a slight buckling. The salon is large, easily accommodating fifty people, and, as our tour guide explains, these were the only homes within the city. Although archaeologists assume that there were smaller houses above these, ascending up and over the crest of the hill, most of the middle and lower classes (if there even was a middle class) lived in cramped, squalid conditions outside the city.

The floors are primarily geometric patterns, featuring red

and dark blue mosaic "carpets" that run the length of the hallways. Marble slabs cling to the interior red brick walls, and a few tables are covered with smaller broken shards being fit together like a puzzle. Some rooms are still so intact we can see frescoed portraits with laurel wreaths painted red and gold. I am looking for signs of Christians—symbols that the early believers used to signify their presence: crosses, fish, the round Ichthys. I want to spot a scene from the Gospels, but I don't think they've been used yet. I think those came later when church buildings became representations of the Bible for the illiterate. I see Roman faces staring up at me, but no Jesus. I wonder what is still uncovered or what will emerge as the puzzle pieces of fragmented walls are put back together.

If history is our modern interpretation of what happened in the past, given the evidence available and the interpreter's perspective, then history is fluid. The more archaeologists discover and the more accessible those discoveries are online, and the more women enter the academy to pursue research of interest to them, the more we rediscover and unlearn previously held beliefs about the role of women in history. Sandra Glahn's study of Artemis is one example. What will we rediscover next?

Women were slowly written out of the early Christian story, even though Jesus brought a revolutionary message. *You are in a patriarchal culture, but I say you are equal. Let me show you… I'll talk to a Samaritan woman alone at a well. I'll let a "sinner" anoint my feet with her tears and oil. I'll forgive a woman caught in adultery. I'll take the money of wealthy women to fund our ministry. I'll have women travel with us. And I'll appear in my newly resurrected body to a woman first.* Jesus was a feminist.

And so was Paul. *There is neither male nor female.* Revolutionary!

Women in the first centuries led the church. They were evangelists (Priscilla), deaconesses (Phoebe), and church leaders (Lydia, Nympha, Apphia). There were no church buildings yet, so believers met in homes—in the domain of women. They didn't hide out in the kitchen with a salon full of people. Men, women, children, and slaves gathered as one—Jew and Greek, slave and free, male and female. When persecution was bad, they worshiped in secret. In areas like Cappadocia, they went underground. But the church grew. It grew faster in those first three centuries than in the subsequent seventeen combined. What was so different, other than the presence of women in leadership?

Constantine changed everything. Peace does not always mean prosperity for all. He Christianized the empire, stopped persecutions, and started a massive building campaign. Grand church buildings would signify his new power, and agreed-upon creeds would unify the people. As the church came out of hiding and into brick and mortar, it began to reflect the culture more and more, and the revolutionary way of Jesus less and less. The hierarchy of bishops and archbishops, the robes and headdresses mimicking those of Jewish priests, the design of the church buildings with the altar behind a holy divide all paralleled temple days. And as the new emperor declared he was God's divine representative on earth, politics and religion were fused and power structures cemented. The Imperial Era had begun. What then to do with the women?

It is not a stretch of imagination to picture house church meetings in these magnificent halls of the Terrace Homes. Where else would they have fit? Any other house would have been large enough for just one family. Only wealthy homes had servants and space and would have qualified as the "church that meets in their home."

Roman culture was patriarchal, but women were mistresses of their private domain. Therefore, it is no surprise that Christian gatherings, which had to be held inside homes (and often secretly), were a) in large enough homes to accommodate more guests than just the family and servants, and b) under the domain of the mistress of the house. This is why we read Paul's greetings to Lydia, Nympha, Apphia, and Priscilla. But this is also why Jesus' way was so counter-cultural.

We first learn of Priscilla and Aquila as some of the Jews expelled from Rome under Emperor Claudius's decree. They have become refugees in the largest city outside of Rome, Corinth, when Paul meets them and begins to work as a tentmaker alongside them.[73] I used to picture canvas lean-tos like you might see in a slum, but their tents were probably made of high-quality leather used by soldiers in Roman military camps. It's quite possible this was a lucrative trade, and they were able to support the church's activities, including serving the widows and the poor. When Paul goes to Ephesus, they join him. Again, I used to picture Paul hitching a ride on ships, but they could probably all afford their own passage on a voyage across the Aegean.[74]

In Ephesus, we meet Apollos, a learned believer and incredible orator, new to town but without the whole Gospel story.

---

73 Acts 18:2

74 Acts 18:18

Priscilla and Aquila fill in the gaps for him, teaching him the rest of the story after the baptism of John. They are mentioned again in Paul's letter to the Corinthians by name, right after he writes that all the churches in the province of Asia greet them, implying that this couple held a vital role in the regional church.[75] And again, in Paul's letter to the Romans (where they returned after Claudius' reign), he thanks them as fellow workers and for risking their lives to save his neck. He even says the entire church of Gentiles should thank them for this![76] In the six verses in which this couple is named, all but two list Priscilla's name first (and those two are related to them as a couple, not ministry leaders). I'm told this matters. It communicates a hierarchy unconventional in those times. More than her husband, Priscilla was the church leader upon whom Paul relied.

I am desperate to find evidence of her and spend hours reading papers and journals from other women who are equally desperate. We know there must be more. If six verses point to such an incredible leader, there is probably far more that was suppressed or doctored. *Was Aquila originally listed alongside her? Was he ever named first? Did she convert in Rome because of Peter's ministry? Was she a wealthy, educated Roman? Could she have authored the book of Hebrews?[77]*

Finding archaeological evidence in Ephesus is a dead end, but there is some possibility in Rome. A seventh-century guide for pilgrims to Rome lists the Catacombs of Priscilla as a site,

---

75 1 Corinthians 16:19

76 Romans 16:3

77 Mimi Haddad, "Priscilla, Author of the Epistle to the Hebrews?," *CBE International*, January 31, 1993, https://www.cbeinternational. org/resource/priscilla-author-epistle-hebrews/

and it is believed that a Priscilla is buried there, among other bodies. In the early days, before widespread persecution, martyrs were used to bolster the faith of the church and often became conflated with different stories, making them even more mythical. Priscilla may have been martyred, or another, later Priscilla, named after her, may have received the honor. Regardless, naming children after her, ascribing martyrdom, and deeming a site holy were all ways that people showed adoration and respect. This is the evidence we have that Priscilla made a significant impact on the church.

As I've written about in Cisterns, the era of women in church leadership waned as the church became institutionalized. Those early years of living out Jesus' teachings, focused on the heart of the Gospel, not the precise way of describing His essence or the Trinity, or who could administer the Eucharist, would come to a close by the fourth century. However, in Ephesus during the first century, we are at the height of Jesus' revolution. It's why we end our pilgrimage here, in the place and in the time period when it's indisputable what Jesus thought of women, when all that he had turned upside down was still evident.

We exit the Terrace Homes and are literally around the corner from the incredible library. Although it was not yet here when Priscilla was (it was completed in 135 CE), I imagine her walking out of her house, past the library, to the agora to listen to whatever Paul is talking about that day. The facade of the library features four alcoves, each housing a statue of a woman embodying a Roman virtue (the current statues are replicas): From left to right, they are Sofia (Wisdom), Arete (Virtue), Ennoia (Insight), and Episteme (Knowledge). I picture Priscilla smiling, recalling lectures from her Roman education and considering how she might incorporate these virtues into a sermon. The learned teacher, church planter, patron, and fellow worker who risked her life to save Paul's neck. I like her so.

> *Are you surprised by anything you've read here about Priscilla? What do you do with Jesus' revolutionary view of women? Have you ever considered that Jesus and Paul were feminists?*

LAHMACUN

Nomads and travelers of the ancient world perfected flat bread, a versatile food that could be prepared ahead of time and used as a base for various toppings on the go. Over time, lahmacun evolved into a thin-crusted conduit of minced lamb, red peppers, and spices—a very thin pizza concept. Sort of. I love lahmacun! It is served with parsley, lemon wedges, and a fresh red onion "salad." Turks roll all of this into the flatbread and eat it like a burrito. They are easy to make if you put some muscle into rolling the dough thin enough. I imagine Priscilla looking for an easy meal during her travels around Rome, Corinth, and Ephesus. Perhaps she, Aquila, and Paul enjoyed something similar together.

1. For the dough, make it simple by using whatever you would typically use for pizza dough, and roll it out extra thin. Preheat the oven to 500 degrees.

2. For the meat mixture, combine ½ lb. ground beef or lamb, ½ cup thinly diced red pepper, ½ cup thinly diced yellow onion, ⅓ cup finely chopped parsley, 2 pressed garlic cloves, 1 teaspoon oregano, 1 teaspoon cumin, ½ teaspoon mint, ½ teaspoon salt, 2 tablespoons red pepper paste (you can sub for tomato paste or make your own if you can't find this in a Mediterranean market), ⅔ cup water. Mix all the ingredients with your hands for 3-5 minutes, squeezing.

3. Your pizzas should be about 6 inches in diameter and placed directly on a baking stone or heavy metal

cooking tray. Press the meat mixture into a very thin layer that covers the dough.

4. Cook for about 7 minutes.

5. Serve with fresh parsley, lemon wedges, and an onion salad: thin slices of onion with sumac and chopped parsley.

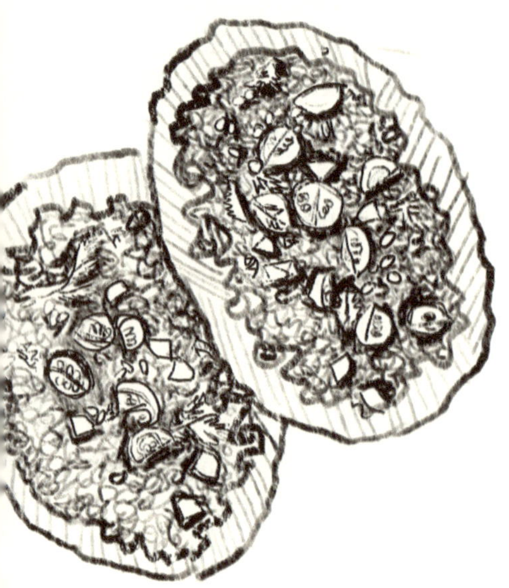

SAINTS

AFTER MY SIXTH grader introduced me to Theodora, I started exploring new places differently. If this incredible woman had left her fingerprints on a city I loved and thought I knew so well, how many women had shaped other places without me ever knowing their names? Now, before I travel anywhere, I try to find several stories of women in history who left their mark on the city. In Bergen, I found a statue, and in Stockholm, I ate in a cafe. In Edinburgh, I found the first women's hospital, and in Nairobi, I found a forest of trees. In Denver, it was the home of the first black female doctor, and in Fez, it was the oldest university in the world.

Every year, I discover more stories of women who shaped Istanbul. They are endless, it would seem: a fountain I passed countless times in the Spice Bazaar, commissioned by the daughter of a sultan; a palace along the Bosphorus belonged to a princess famous for poetry; a Byzantine church named after a woman uncovered beneath the mall I frequented most. But I have been challenged to find more stories of women who shaped Ephesus. There must be more than the Amazonians, Artemis, Virgin Mary, and Priscilla!

History remembers women of power or scandal. So, we know of queens and empresses, and we know of the women who caused problems, either by their stubborn faith or their "sexual deviancy." In the church, devoid of position or publication, women were remembered through sainthood. I believe that the only means available to acknowledge outstanding female leadership, sacrifice, miracles, teaching, or martyrdom was to venerate them. As a non-Catholic, I confess this was an odd thing until I found myself in a Cappadocian chapel studying the frescoed faces of haloed men and women and realized they were merely people whose stories were immortalized in the only way the church knew how.

And so, I started my search for more women in Ephesus by looking for saints. Which is to say, the Catholics and Orthodox led me.

Hermione was one of Philip's four unmarried daughters who prophesied.[78] Philip, as a little reminder, was one of the seven chosen to care for widows and was the same Philip who cast demons out of people in Samaria and the same one who evangelized and baptized the Ethiopian on the road from Jerusalem to Gaza.[79] It is debated whether this Philip was the same as Philip the Apostle. However, for our purposes, what is essential is that he had four daughters gifted with prophesy, one of whom was named Hermione, and she traveled with her sister to Ephesus to continue her theological studies under John.

---

78 Acts 21:9

79 Acts 6:5; Acts 8:4-8; Acts 8:26-40

I have come to read the stories of saints with a grin. What is legend, and what is truth? Are they not a combination of both, and is not the fantastical but a literary means of telling us in this modern age how incredible they must have been? I no longer care how real the story is. What it tells me is that they existed and were amazing. This is how the church remembered Hermione.

Hermione was known for the healing arts and started a hostel in Ephesus for the poor and sick. Perhaps this was situated around a fabled healing mineral spring? I know of one in Heiropolis, nearer to Laodicea than Ephesus. I have swum in the warm waters above fallen columns of that Greek city. Hermione was a faithful Christian in an era when faithful Christians were an annoyance to Pliny the Younger, the governor of the region at the time. He wrote to the Emperor Trajan about the "contagion" of Christianity, and it is the first record of Rome that differentiates between Judaism and Christianity.[80] Pliny asked Trajan for permission to torture Christian women to get them to recant (all recorded by the famous historian, Josephus). This suggests that women were incredibly influential and powerful during this time in the newly recognized religious movement known as Christianity.

Trajan visited Ephesus. We know this because across from the Terrace Homes is an ornate fountain dedicated to his arrival in the city. He summoned Hermione and attempted to force her to deny Christ, which she did not. Instead, she prophesied his defeat of the Parthians and that his son-in-law, Hadrian,

---

80 Pliny the Younger, *Letters*, vol. 2: *Books 8–10. Panegyricus*, trans. Betty Radice (Cambridge, MA: Harvard University Press, 1969), 10.96.9.

would succeed him in 117 CE. Liking this prophecy, Trajan let her go. Then, when Hadrian indeed took the throne and learned of her prophecy, *he* summoned her. Orthodox tradition tells us that Hadrian asked her age, and she gave a cheeky reply: "Christ knows how old I am and where I come from."[81] For her obstinacy, he punished her by dipping her naked body into a cauldron of boiling metal! But, protected by angels, she emerged unscathed. Shocked, he dipped his hand in the pot, and his skin and nails fell right off. Enraged, he had her thrown into fire, but the fire engulfed everyone around her instead. At this point, she feigned repentance and asked to go sacrifice to the idols. Relieved, he sent her off with guards to a pagan temple, but while she was praying, all of the statues in the temple were destroyed! Finally, Hadrian had her taken out of the city to be executed, and the executioners' hands were paralyzed, and then they converted. Hermione lived to see another day.

This miraculous and somewhat hard-to-believe story is called hagiography—the art of magnifying a saint's life to the degree that anything less than reverence is impossible. How could you do anything but honor Hermione as a saint when hearing a story such as this?

Saint or no, miraculous escape or no, here is what I understand: Philip's daughter wanted to learn more about following Jesus and left home to do so. She followed in his footsteps and started a ministry to help the poor and sick. She garnered enough attention to get on the Emperor's radar as a threat to

---

81   Hippolyte   Delehaye,   ed.,   Synaxarium   Ecclesiae Constantinopolitanae: e Codice Sirmondiano nunc Berolinensi, adiectis synaxariis selectis (Brussels: Société des Bollandistes, 1902), s.v. "Septembris 4: Ἑρμιόνη.

the empire, along with lots of other women in this new religion, causing more disruption to Rome than the Jews ever had. God protected her through multiple attempts on her life, and she is remembered today in both the Catholic and Orthodox traditions as a saint.

I'll remember her as I walk by the Temple of Hadrian and the Fountain of Trajan as the woman who said *How dare you ask my age* to the Roman Emperor and as the woman who survived a concerted effort to snuff out the influence of Christian women in the empire. When we visit the Terrace Homes, I'll linger on the surrounding hillside where she and many Christians are thought to be buried. And the next time I visit the hot springs in Hierapolis, I'll remember her as one who adventured away from home to serve the least of these. I'll remind myself that sainthood is a gift of history if nothing else.

I have entered the land of sanctified imagination—a term Wilda Gaffney describes as "the fertile creative space where the preacher-interpreter enters the text."[82] It has led to a more generous reading of scripture and allowed the possibility of uncovering more truth. Particularly, following the path of saints in a tradition otherwise foreign to me reveals names and stories outlined in books I never would have read. The *Acts of Paul and Thecla*, a section in the text of *The Acts of Paul*, is one such non-canonical book.

Thought to be authored in the mid-second century, only

---

82 Wilda Gafney, *The Womanist Midrash: A Reintroduction to the Women of the Torah and the Throne* (Louisville, KY: Westminster John Knox Press, 2017), 3.

fragments of the entire book exist, but complete copies of the section *Paul and Thecla* exist in multiple languages as far back as the third century, suggesting it was widely circulated. No wonder, since it was written in non-academic Greek and in the style of a romance novel of the time. However, I imagine its popularity was mainly due to the protagonist—a rebellious young woman who defied everyone's expectations, becoming a patron saint of women's empowerment.

Thecla's story is somewhat similar to Hermione's. She was miraculously spared from death multiple times, despite the Roman fury directed against her. However, there is actually much more historical evidence to support her life and legend. Thecla was betrothed to be married to an important official in Iconium (present-day Konya, Turkey) when Paul entered the town on his first missionary journey. From her open bedroom window, Thecla remained for three days straight, so enraptured by Paul's sermons that neither her mother nor her betrothed could tear her away. Concluding that the marriage was off, and Thecla would follow Paul's preaching around virginity, they turned her in to the governor (Roman law at the time required women to marry and bear children, and penalized celibacy). I suspect she was sentenced to death for the dual insult of refusing to marry a nobleman, the reason being her faith in Jesus.

Thecla survived a burning at the stake, met up with Paul, who was hiding with other Christians in caves outside the city, and traveled with him to Antioch. There, a nobleman tried to take her for his own, and upon her refusal, also gave her to the governor to be killed. She was sentenced to death by beasts in an arena where she survived a lioness, a bear, and vicious water animals. When the tank of water appeared, she got in and said, "In your name, O my Lord Jesus Christ, I am this last day baptized," and the women in the stands went wild, rushing to her with fragrant oils to ward off the beasts and protect her. Thecla survived because her patroness, Trifina, died from all the drama which distracted the attention of high-ranking officials, thus concluding the death scene:

> Then the women cried out together with a loud voice, and with one accord gave praise unto God and said: There is but one God, who is the God of Thecla; the one God who has delivered Thecla. Their voices were so loud that the whole city seemed to be shaken, and Trifina herself heard the glad tidings and arose again, and ran with the multitude to meet Thecla; and embracing her said: Now I believe there will be a resurrection of the dead; now I am persuaded that my daughter is alive. Come home with me, my daughter Thecla, and I will turn over all that I have to you.[83]

Escaping death, Thecla found Paul again and told him that God had assisted in her baptism, and she was called to preach. Paul blessed her to go and share the Gospel in the area, which she did, performing miracles and healing, and gathering many women to her side in a monastic-like community. She spent her remaining years in a cave that, by the early fourth century, was known as the Holy Grotto of Thecla.

She preached the word and baptized, and Paul blessed it. This may be why Tertullian condemned *The Acts of Paul and Thecla* in 200 CE, and why it seemed like a contradiction to the

---

83 *The Acts of Paul and Thecla*, chap. 9, in *The Apocryphal New Testament*, trans. M. R. James (Oxford: Clarendon Press, 1924).

same Paul who wrote that women should be silent; why it was not included in the New Testament canon, and why its authorship was doubted. But here's the thing: The book may be an embellishment, an early feminist story that centers Thecla, her patroness, and the women in the arena. There may be much in it that is false (did a lioness really bow at her feet?), but Thecla was real. Other historians of the time wrote about her, and theologians honored her.

Our Cappadocian heroes of the fourth century were well acquainted with Thecla. Gregory of Nazianzus, a friend of Macrina and her brothers, spent five years in Thecla's community before becoming a famous orator and Bishop of Hagia Sophia. And Gregory of Nyssa wrote that his mother, Emmelia, had a vision during labor that she was to secretly name Macrina after Thecla as a foreshadowing of her life and leadership:

> At her first confinement, she became the mother of Macrina. When the due time came for her pangs to be ended by delivery, she fell asleep and seemed to be carrying in her hands that which was still in her womb. And someone in form and raiment more splendid than a human being appeared and addressed the child she was carrying by the name of Thecla, that Thecla, I mean, who is so famous among the virgins. After doing this and testifying to it three times, he departed from her sight and gave her easy delivery, so that at that moment she awoke from sleep and saw her dream realised. Now this name was used only in secret. But it seems to me that the apparition spoke not so much to guide the mother to a right choice of name, as to forecast the life of the young child, and to indicate by

the name that she would follow her namesake's mode of life.[84]

A woman most famous among the virgins. Read: a woman whose only agency was her body. To be a devoted Christ-follower required a vow of virginity in a culture that demanded marriage and childbirth. And an entire community of women flocked to her, and to Macrina, and to the women of the desert who unwittingly sacrificed their humanity to achieve holiness.

On a recent trip to Turkey with my husband, I visit ancient Iconium in search of Thecla's fingerprints. Not far from the modern-day city of Konya is a small community divided by a river; on one side is a hill pocketed with caves, on the other, wooden houses once populated by Greek residents. At the end of the little valley sits one of the oldest Byzantine churches (327 CE) in continual use until 1924. Recall Constantine's mother, Helena, whose own pilgrimage led to the building of churches on sacred sites throughout the region. I posited that perhaps it was she who gave Macrina the Younger a fragment of the cross found in her necklace when she died. The road from Jerusalem to Constantinople passed through Iconium, and I imagine when she arrived, Helena heard all about the iconic woman who was miraculously spared from death and fled town to meet up with Paul, hiding with Christians in the nearby caves. As

---

84 Gregory of Nyssa, *Life of St. Macrina*, trans. [Translator], in *Nicene and Post-Nicene Fathers*, 1st ser., vol. 5, ed. Philip Schaff (Peabody, MA: Hendrickson Publishers, 1916), 17–79, https://www.tertullian.org/fathers/gregory_macrina_1_life.htm.

was Helena's custom, she built a church here to memorialize the sacred and holy. And, while there is no evidence of Thecla or Helena in the recently renovated Church of Aya Elena (Saint Helena), Thecla's regional fame is documented.

Up and over the crest behind Helena's church, I find a cave church. The cross-shaped interior, defined by a narthex, nave, and altar, remains, despite the vandalized walls and trash heaps. I imagine Thecla showing up, breathless from jogging all the way from the site of the failed stake-burning to the secret cave only Christians knew of. Paul is inside, maybe leading a service of lament, for surely they thought she had perished. Did she rush in and announce the miracle? Did she hover in the entry-way, waiting for a dramatic moment? Was there an embrace, and if so, friendly or romantic? Or perhaps the most realistic question, *at this point, did Paul even know who she was?*

I would later discover that in Ephesus, from the far end of the Roman street that connects the amphitheater to the harbor, up the rocky hill, is a locked cave. With special permission, one can enter and see the fifth-century frescoes that remain. Paul is painted there, in the act of preaching with his balding head so precisely detailed in the *Acts of Paul and Thecla.* To his right is a woman, Theocleia, the infamous mother who betrayed her own daughter in our story. And to his left is a woman in a window, Thecla.

Of course, I had no idea this cave existed in all my trips to Ephesus. Just like I never knew the story of Thecla. I want to know why it matters so much to me, to find their stories. To keep finding them. And I realize it's their humanity I'd like to reclaim. I want to bring them down off the walls, to remove the sainthood and breathe the fullness of life back into their story. Who are you, Thecla, really?

If one were to immortalize you as a saint, what might it be for? How would history best remember you? What does it mean to learn the story of someone like Thecla? What does it bring up for you regarding women's roles in the Church?

ÇOBAN SALATISI

TO HONOR HERMIONE and Thecla, we must have Shepherd's Salad, a light mix of diced tomatoes, diced skinned cucumbers, chopped parsley, olive oil, salt, and a bit of lemon juice. As shepherds of the women who followed after them, it seems fitting to prepare this simple dish. Just toss it together and serve cold with a side of thick pide bread (focaccia is a good substitute).

SEA

I AM NOT a water person, but I have a hard time leaving the Aegean Sea. Every year, I say goodbye to our group here and linger another twenty-four hours, occupying a lounge chair for an entire day with a front row seat to the rolling blue waves.

The year I learn that *raqia*, the firmament God created on Day Two, was like a dome over the earth, I am in one of these chairs. The water is before me, an endless expanse that fills 70% of the surface of this round home that sustains and nourishes us. I picture the vaulted domed Turkish bath, which felt so womb-like this time.

One of the women this year shared a story of a dark time when the community pool tended to her grief. Every morning, she would swim laps until her tears ceased, and she would emerge from the water able to endure another day. For some, the water comforts, restores. Another woman rented a jet ski on our personal retreat day. She needed to play with something that had always felt safe and had recently been beckoning. For some, the water is kind and inviting. Personally, I cannot calm myself if I can't see what swims beneath. My heart races as I perceive every sensation to be a flesh-eating fish seeking to devour. And the strength of the waves is unnerving. For me, the water of the Aegean is too powerful.

My husband has posted four words above his office door: bigger, stronger, wiser, kinder. They remind him, and all who sit with him, of who God is. This comes to mind as I force myself to cool off in the salty water. Like God, the sea is bigger, stronger, wiser, kinder. The sea is what we each need it to be, taking shape to fill our longing for comfort, play, or power.

On Day Two, the firmament waters were broken, and there was land and there was sea: *raqia*. I do not know Hebrew, but surely it is related to *rakhum*? In Exodus 34:6, the first time God describes himself, he says *I am compassionate*, using the Hebrew *rakhum*, which means womb. Tracy has told me that the word used in Genesis 1:6 for the firmament over the earth is *raqia*, also illustrating a womb whose waters ruptured. The waters break and life begins. This is who God tells us he is: like a womb. Like a mother.

This is the year I will return home to an empty house, to the completion of a full quarter of a century of motherhood. And, while I do not yet know how frequently the tears will come, I already have a sense of needing God's mothering. I have noticed the womb metaphor everywhere on this pilgrimage, but especially as I lay on the lounge chair staring at something that feels more powerful than me. It scares me, but I desperately want its strength and containment, its nourishment and restorative energy. I want to be mothered in this season of transition, so much so that I dare to enter the powerful waters by myself.

The sun is starting to set on the intention I've had all day: to brave the sea alone and bring back a vial as a remembrance of God's mothering. The longer I have stalled, the rougher the waves have become, but I am too stubborn to abandon the plan. Bigger, stronger, *and* wiser, kinder. I enter the Aegean, the womb of God, and I surrender to the unknown. I release the beginning of what will become a deluge of grief. I bear my fear for as long as I can, and I emerge with a bottle of seawater to remember.

⌁

There is more, and it takes a different body of raging waves and processing with my metaphor-loving husband to locate it. Weeks later, we are at another beach, on our "victory lap" trip, planned almost a year in advance, celebrating our status as empty nesters. I am again in awe of the power and strength of the sea, and I still have no desire to go in. After rattling off the rivers, lakes, and oceans that have borne witness to some of my fondest memories, I am aware that in all of these memories, I am never *in* the water, but near, next to, listening, observing.

It's dark, and we're sipping wine from a thermos in a quiet cabana, taking in the sounds of the waves. Unbeknownst to us when we booked, this week is more of a memorial trip than a victory lap. We are so sad.

I ask him, "What do you make of the womb, water, and mothering of God I've been pondering?"

"Well, you should probably figure out the actual Hebrew of those two words. Are they truly connected?" he says.

"Yeah, sure. But they're probably not. I would have found something by now. I'm forcing it. I meant the water. The sea. My *need* to enter it. Why do you think it pulled me so, on this year's pilgrimage?"

He says, "What did you need from it—this time?"

I sit in silence for a bit before wondering aloud, "I guess

I needed someone, something, stronger and more powerful. I needed to feel my fear."

He pours some more wine as I hold up the phone flashlight and finish my churro. My mind is at the Aegean hotel—that day by myself as I relaxed in the lounge chair, weakened by food poisoning again. Two years in a row, each time shockingly violent.

"And I always vomit *there*. I'm never sick like that, but for two years, there at *that* hotel, like something needed to purge from my body."

"So, you come to the water, the womb of God, and you have morning sickness," he proposes. "And this time, you miscarried."

I have a tingling sensation, and my heart pounds as the truth of this metaphor hits me.

"The sea that day, by myself, was my mikvah," I whisper.

"And you emerged purified."

"But the violence of the vomit, in the middle of the whole restaurant! It's like my body was screaming: Too much grief! And death," I say. Scenes from the last few months rush by: betrayal, loss, disappointment, failure. Not *only* did a season of parenting end, but other pains related to decisions I had made in our business that backfired, as well as some unexpected difficulties on the trip to Turkey.

"I thought I was birthing new life again, but it died. All of it. And all at once."

I picture myself alone in the lounge chair for hours, writing and intermittently looking up at the Aegean. Was I trembling that day? My stomach was still weakened by the violent expulsion of the night before, and I was so confused, scared, and sad about what I would return to the next day at work. I went into the sea so my body could feel her fear. I went in because God invited me to feel the strength and power of a mother's heart.

I think about the year before's food poisoning, vomiting over the sea's edge, while Tracy rubbed my back. The next day, at her urging, we went to get my Theodora tattoo. That year, I carried new life to term and birthed a beautiful new perspective as I returned to America and a new role in our business. I remember walking into our house and removing the Saran Wrap covering my new mark. My husband's first question: "What does her name mean?" How did I not know? The *actual* Greek meaning of Theodora? "God's gift," he said a minute later, putting his phone down and smiling.

In the dark cabana, my mind returns to these waves and the present. I shake my head and say, "This is what you do to your clients, yeah?"

He says, "The waters break, and birth happens. And it happens at the Charisma."

We look at each other. How did it not occur to me? The name of my favorite hotel means *God's grace.*

The Charisma is located ten miles south of the ancient port of Ephesus, which, in the mid-first century, was one of the largest cities in the known world. The grand Temple of Artemis would have been visible from the harbor as multitudes of pilgrims disembarked. The virgin goddess drove the economy, and from the sea came her consumers until the saucy new Jewish sect disrupted business and worship.

It is widely believed that the apostle to whom Jesus entrusted the care of his mother is the same author of Revelation, written in exile on the nearby Roman penal colony, the island of

Patmos. Some traditions maintain John brought Mary with him when he relocated to Ephesus, that he brought the Virgin Mary to the city of the virgin goddess. But was she the only woman on the boat?

Seven seemingly distinct Marys are named in the New Testament, and it is challenging to differentiate them. Mary (the English version of the Hebrew Miriam) was the most popular girl's name in ancient Judea, and there were three who appear to be closest to Jesus. Mary, his mother, Mary her sister, wife of Clopas (perhaps Joseph's brother), and Mary Magdalene were all standing near the cross when Jesus charged John to take care of the one who was his mother.[85] Perhaps John escorted her directly from the cross that evening because only Mary Magdalene and "the other Mary" were at the tomb that night and again the next morning.

History tells us that these Jesus followers were viewed as a disruptive Jewish sect in the Roman-Hebrew status quo. The Jews were so distressed that they put these three Marys (and other followers) on a sail-less, oar-less boat out to sea. Some say Mary Magdalene ended up in Rome and even held an audience with the Emperor Tiberius. Perhaps she is the Mary thanked for her hard labor in Paul's list of twenty-nine believers he names in the letter to the Romans. Some say she went to the south of France and preached through the whole province with Maxim, one of the seventy-two disciples, before spending the last thirty years of her life in contemplation in a cave. It is believed that her relics were discovered in 1279 and are viewable today in St. Maximin-la-Sainte-Baume. Most say "the other Mary" was with

---

85 John 19:25

her. This Mary is mentioned seven times in the New Testament, more than many of the apostles. I like to picture it: three Marys traveling the sea, timid of the Aegean's strength and power as well.

Seven women shared the most popular name of the time. Why? I mean, *why Mary*?

English: Mary
Roman: Maria
Greek: Mariam
Aramaic: Maryam
Hebrew: Miriam

Mary, mother of Jesus, wasn't a "thing" yet. She didn't officially become "Mother of God: Theotokos" until the Council of Ephesus in 431 CE. Who were all of those Marys named after? Certainly not the cheeky and controversial sister of Herod. But there is another Miriam the Hebrews certainly knew. The one named in Micah 6:3-4, in God's testimony of how good He has been to Israel, that he gave them not just Moses, not just Aaron, but Miriam, too. The actual savior of the Hebrews was a desperate and brave older sister who negotiated for the life of her innocent baby brother with an Egyptian princess. The one who led the Israelites through the Red Sea with singing while Moses held his arms outstretched, keeping the waters at bay. The first woman to be called a prophetess. The midwife of the Hebrews, leading them to new life in the promised land via the birth canal of the parting sea.

Mary. Maryam. Miriam. From Mer, a name with an Egyptian origin story. Whose brothers were also given Egyptian names. Mer, from the Egyptian *beloved*. Or possibly Mar, meaning *rebellious,* and Yam meaning, and I cannot make this up, *sea.*

On top of Mount Sinai, God proclaims his name to Moses: "I am the Lord." And, for the first time, describes himself. I am the "womb-like one." My compassion is like a womb: generative, embodied, sheltering, and, in its essence, maternal. *This is the first description we receive of the one who has led them through the parting waters of the Red Sea and will one day lead them through the Jordan River and will eventually come to them through the physical womb of Miriam.*

One Miriam who birthed the salvation of a nation; another Miriam who birthed salvation itself.

And the waters break, and there is life. We are born of the waters.

> *What do you do when you need your body to feel, release, or process something? What is your relationship with the water? How does the metaphor of womb, birth, and mothering speak to you?*

RAKI: ASLAN SÜTLÜ

RAKI, AN ANISE-FLAVORED liquor, is the national drink of Turkey. The go-to drink for celebrating anything and everything, Turks drink Rakı with a meze of feta and fresh melon, followed by fish (it's a whole thing). The waiter pours it into tall, slim glasses and then pours cold water over it (about half and half). The clear liquid turns a milky white, and voila, lion's milk (aslan sütlü), the symbol for strength, courage, and camaraderie. You'll need strength to enter the waters and brave new life. Clink the bottom of another's glass and toast, Şerefe!

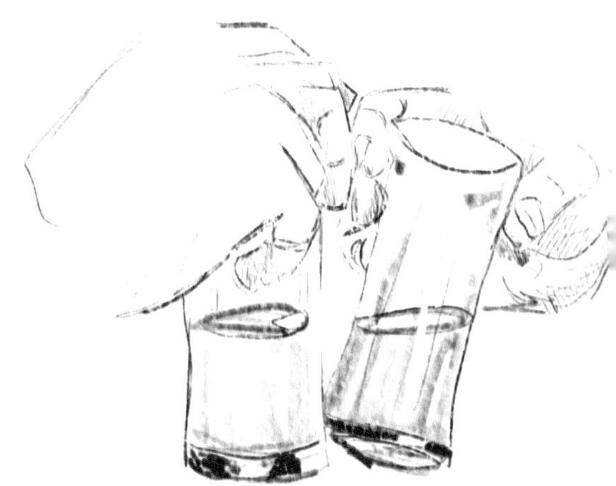

CONCLUSION

PILGRIMAGE

I BELIEVE IN pilgrimages. Returning to the places in which we were forged. Blessing our younger selves and letting them off the hook. Celebrating and grieving and marking.

On a hot day in July, our minivan finishes the I-80 slog it has been on for the previous fourteen hours and heads north on Lake Shore Drive. Three kids complain in the back, the middle with her broken leg propped atop a cooler. We will not let a wheelchair deter us from a planned trip down memory lane: to show them where we met and to speak at the church from which we launched into ministry.

I sit silently in the passenger seat, fighting nostalgic tears, remembering the eighteen-year-old from Virginia and all her big-city dreams. At first, the ones to get rich, and later, as her faith grew, the ones to change lives. We show the kids the pizza place where we met, look for the spot where our names are in graffiti. We walk the path upon which we fell in love, stand beneath the window where it was first spoken.

We steal a few hours alone and remember those two principled and naive kids who thought they might change the world.

With weathered and broken hearts, matured and aged, we offer them kindness. We bless their marital mission statement and laugh at their arrogance. We are grateful to them for their vision and determination. They came to the city as children with singular ambition and left as a unified force that would be crucial for the next chapter. We are so very thankful.

It is another hot day in July, two years later, when we show our kids what the next chapter held. It is a bigger city with bigger stakes: Istanbul. They were once there, even if they don't remember it all, and so we show them the hospitals and playgrounds, school yards and kiddie areas in malls, the places we haunted, where I spent hours trying to survive as a young mom. We ride ferries and buses and trolleys and trains, and they bless me: "Mom, you were badass." I didn't realize how much I needed that blessing until I received it.

I look up at the fifth-story balcony on which I filled a kiddie pool and entertained a one-year-old on a hot July day seventeen years prior. *I see you.* I walk past the windows behind which we had an awkward mediation with coworkers. *I see you.* We buy a pastry in the bakery, which was open that night when my husband was stabbed. *I see you. And I release you. Breathe again.*

Again, we steal a few hours for ourselves. This time with more tears and a little less laughter, as we can still feel the weight of parenting, leading, and loving in this place. The city to which we brought all of our principles and plans only to be eviscerated, spit out with nothing more than a battered faith. And so, we gather up our younger, bruised selves and honor their sacrifice. We bless their hope. Name their courage. And mark that which survived.

We look at each other, to each other. We *did* this. And *we* survived. There is grief for sure, but also gratitude. Because of it all, we became who we are. Our marriage is what it is. We gather up the tattered threads of all the story trails that only he and I will ever fully know. It's neither pretty nor complete, but we remember. And that is important.

Because the story of a marriage is forged in the crucible of tattered threads, bruised hope, and weathered dreams, and sometimes, we need to make a pilgrimage to remember.

The *Lost Women of Turkey Pilgrimage* ends at a lovely hotel on the Aegean Sea, nestled in a bay with rope hammocks hanging over the turquoise blue and balconies that face the sunset. After a long day of walking on the brutal marble Roman roads, we conclude our journey with a silent retreat day. It has been a whirlwind and transformative trip, and before the demands of family and work bombard us again, we need to mark what has transpired in our souls.

The concept of marking is ancient. God instructed the Israelites to erect a tower of stones in remembrance of what he did for them at the Jordan River. Circumcision and baptism are forms of marking oneself or one's child as belonging to God. Graduation ceremonies, weddings, and funerals are all formalized marking events. As a people, we are in need of remembrance.

Throughout our journey, we have invited the women to pay attention to their stories, to see hidden and tucked away places in their hearts through a new lens, to locate themselves in the place or circumstances of the women we "meet." We have also invited them to be on the lookout for a symbol of the trip—something they might buy and take back to remember. A coin, for one. A necklace for another. For me? A tattoo.

God has been at work in each of our lives so uniquely, so lovingly. He is answering questions we didn't know we carried and tending to places we weren't aware were still raw. He has shown himself in the hamam and the nargile, in the caves and the barren desert landscape. And for her who still waits for God to reveal himself, there is the sea. The water envelopes her body, and her spirit floats. This last day is for her.

The year I mark my journey with a permanent tattoo of Theodora's monogram is a huge one for me. It's not about the tattoo (though it's my first), or the Turkish artists who have no idea what or who I'm trying to describe, or the tattered black leather couch we sit on in the empty studio while the tattoo parlor down the street is lively and crowded. I've already made up my mind, and that feels final for me. What took five decades to arrive at is far more significant.

Theodora opened up the world to me. Discovering her existence, her story, and her fingerprints with my twelve-year-old daughter felt sacred and whimsical. God was awakening me to more of who he created me to be: curious, a lover of history, a curator of the feminine story. For years, I let Theodora guide me. As I considered the fullness of her story and embraced the complexity of her humanity, I was in awe of what I was realizing about myself.

David Brenner writes, "Deep knowledge of God and deep knowing of self always develop interactively."[86] I knew God was leading me closer to Him through a deeper understanding of

---

86 David G. Benner, *The Gift of Being Yourself: The Sacred Call to Self-Discovery* (Downers Grove, IL: InterVarsity Press, 2004), 31.

myself. Year after year, Turkey creates this space for my soul to expand, for me to hear from Him in ways I only do in this place. In preparation for the trip, I had been gleaning wisdom from Macrina Wiederkehr: "In order to experience healing, it is imperative that we find the courage to look upon our wounds and integrate them into our lives."[87] And so, I entered Turkey ready to attune to the wounds that still needed integration. The first one whispered to me within hours of landing.

As familiar as Turkey is, I will always be a foreigner. In Turkish, the word *yabanci* can mean everything from "of another nationality" to "not from our town." And yet, even though Turks use it among themselves, I used to hear it whispered as I walked by with my blond, curly-haired toddler or decidedly spoken to another as an explanation of why they couldn't understand me. It made me feel othered, as if I were destined to never belong, despite my efforts to excel in language and culture. I came to despise the word. Foreigner. This time, upon arrival, hearing it again stirred my soul in a different way. *Yabanci* originates from the word *yaban*, meaning "outside the community." It can also mean the "wilderness." Look up some synonyms in Turkish, and you'll find *bilinmeyen*, "one who cannot be known."

I know this word deep in my bones. Long before I stood alone on Turkish playgrounds or missed the punch line of jokes or humor in idioms, I knew the loneliness that comes from being outside the community. Age ten, Rockford Elementary: The daily recess terror of getting a role in "house" with the group of girls I longed to befriend. Age eleven, Alcoa Elementary: Would anyone look and smile at me as we passed like train cars

---

87 Macrina Wiederkehr, *Behold Your Life: A Pilgrimage Through Your Memories* (Notre Dame, IN: Sorin Books, 2000), 12.

to the adjacent class in our progressive open classroom concept? Age twelve, middle school number one: Would I pass the cool-enough-to-belong test in my homemade Bermuda shorts? Middle school number two: If running leads to friends, I guess I'm joining the Track Team? Middle school number three: Will this rich group of girls forgive my clearance rack dress from The Limited, so obviously *last year*?

Five schools in five years, and I know the wilderness like I know my own shadow. I learned to wear it well and hustled hard to adapt. Living outside the community became unbearable, and I have only God to thank for the fact that I didn't make horrible decisions to fit in. But though I eventually made friends in each school, I did not escape unscathed. The lie I came to believe and live out is that I naturally belong *on the outside*. People view me as other, unknowable, as *bilinmeyen*.

The story keeps repeating itself, year upon year. It becomes the hermeneutic through which I interpret the world. In high school, I am the good girl with party friends. My first adult job is as the white girl in a black community on the West side of Chicago. After work, I'm a suburbanite doing urban youth ministry. By the time I'm on a campus team led by a Turk in the largest unreached city in the world, I have wholly owned *yabanci*. I am quintessentially outside the community.

I don't start to name this theme until I am fraying at the edges—when my fortified, impenetrable coat of protection has failed to do its job. And I'm long gone from Turkey. For years, I have built a human trafficking prevention response in my county. I work among tough cops, survivors, and johns. The day I participate in a John Sting (trying to "catch" men who buy sex), I sit in a van with the cops and have an epiphany: *What in the world am I doing?* I see the look of shame in the eyes of the johns, and I know I am finally done. I pay attention to how thin I have become, and within months, I am ready to walk away from the entire movement. And the thing I keep asking myself is why have I put myself in the wilderness, outside the community, to be a *yabanci, again?*

Weeks after the John Sting, I find Theodora's mark in the Hagia Sophia with my daughter, the first sign on a journey of restorying this belief of who I am.[88] The former prostitute who found herself Empress of Byzantium, who opened up Metanoia, a shelter for women leaving sex work, used by God to awaken me to more of myself. Here was a woman who was about as far on the outside as they come, leaving her mark on this magnificent church for 1,500 years! Finding her fingerprints begins a journey for me. The wear and tear of being a perpetual outsider finally leads me to explore the story I've been believing: that it's where I am destined to stay. *But what if it's not?*

I work on this for years in the background of my life. It gets better; I become more aware of these feelings when they pop up, but it still pops up. When I hear *yabanci* this time, I am attuned to the stirring inside; I currently feel this way about a situation at home, and it's been eating me up. Theodora has become a friend and a sister to me over the years. In the Orthodox tradition, a patron saint is an advocate or an intercessor, and though I am not Orthodox, I have claimed Theodora as my own. I like to think she is my mentor, interceding for me in heaven. Returning to the little church where she hid eight bishops or the grand church columns upon which her monogram remains,

---

88 At ReStory Counseling, we use this term to capture our approach. In essence, it's a journey to discover the story beneath the one I came to believe.

I am struck by how she, too, remained an outsider despite her influence on the empire. As a Miaphysite in a Chalcedonian era and marriage, her choice to hide the bishops who agreed with her was complete defiance. I am even more drawn to her complexity.

When I consider the incarnation, holy piercing humanity, I realize Jesus also knows what it is to be a *yabanci*. With these two as my guides, I feel a more profound peace with my story. Yes, I have known the wilderness of being outside the community, but I am not *bilinmeyen*. I am also deeply knowable, known, and knowing. I have influence and defiance. I hold holiness and humanity within. I am both/and. And I am ready to mark this settledness on my body.

Theodora's monogram on my wrist signifies the integration of the wound that leads to healing. It also celebrates the complexity of life and all the layers that are a part of me. I have another journey to Turkey to thank for this deeper layer of exploration of my soul. It's why I'll keep returning.

The very design of a pilgrimage invites us to play with metaphor, become aware through landscape, and consider our own story through the lens of another. The one who needs the sea and the one who needs the desert find more of themselves in these places. The one who needs mothering receives it from other participants. The one who needs to forgive Paul and reclaim her voice finds it on the marble road through an ancient city. And all of these paths lead to God, whose voice echoes through the cave church walls and between the great mosques of Sultanahmet, through the stories of ancient women and those told on a rooftop of kilim pillows and carpets.

A pilgrimage is a way of praying with your feet. You go on a pilgrimage because you know there's something missing inside your soul and the only way you can find it is to go to sacred places, places where God made himself known to others. In sacred places, something gets done to you that you've been unable to do yourself.[89]

Our lives are also sacred texts from which we learn more of ourselves and, in turn, more of the divine. Sometimes, these texts come more fully alive in a place that evokes our senses, our memories, and our desires. And often, the pilgrim has very little idea that what she wonders most will be answered on the dusty cobblestone of an ancient land. She returns home with a more profound sense of self and an intense longing to do it all again. If she's like me, she will be back.

Again and again.

---

89 Ian Morgan Cron, *Chasing Francis: A Pilgrim's Tale* (Grand Rapids, MI: Zondervan, 2013), 42.

As I mentioned in the introduction, I am not a trained historian or seminarian. But over the years, I have collected, read, and found helpful the titles below. Sometimes just one paragraph opens an entirely new line of inquiry, and always there are more women's stories to uncover.

Christian History

Bailey, Kenneth E. *Jesus through Middle Eastern Eyes: Cultural Studies in the Gospels*. Downers Grove, IL: IVP Academic, 2008.

Barr, Beth Allison. *The Making of Biblical Womanhood: How the Subjugation of Women Became Gospel Truth*. Grand Rapids, MI: Brazos Press, 2021.

Glahn, Sandra. *Nobody's Mother: Artemis of the Ephesians in Antiquity and the New Testament*. Downers Grove, IL: IVP Academic, 2023.

González, Justo L. *The Story of Christianity, Volume 1: The Early Church to the Dawn of the Reformation*. Rev. and updated ed. New York: HarperOne, 2010.

Gregory of Nyssa. *The Life of Saint Macrina*. Translated by Kevin Corrigan. Eugene, OR: Wipf and Stock, 2005.

Gregory of Nyssa. *On the Soul and the Resurrection*. Translated by

Catharine P. Roth. Crestwood, NY: St. Vladimir's Seminary Press, 1993.

Gupta, Nijay K. *Tell Her Story: How Women Led, Taught, and Ministered in the Early Church*. Downers Grove, IL: IVP Academic, 2023.

McKechnie, Paul. *The First Christian Centuries: Perspectives on the Early Church*. Downers Grove, IL: IVP Academic, 2001.

Sunberg, Carla D. *The Cappadocian Mothers: Deification Exemplified in the Writings of Basil, Gregory and Gregory*. Eugene, OR: Pickwick, 2021.

Swan, Laura. *The Forgotten Desert Mothers: Sayings, Lives, and Stories of Early Christian Women*. New York: Paulist Press, 2001.

Watterson, Meggan. *Mary Magdalene Revealed: The First Apostle, Her Feminist Gospel & the Christianity We Haven't Tried Yet*. *Carlsbad*, CA: Hay House, 2019.

Wilkinson, Rosamund. *Christian Women in Turkey: A History*. London: SPCK, 2023.

Byzantine / Ottoman/ Turkish History

Herrin, Judith. *Unrivalled Influence: Women and Empire in Byzantium*. Princeton: Princeton University Press, 2013.

Hughes, Bettany. *Istanbul: A Tale of Three Cities*. New York: Da Capo Press, 2017.

Kinzer, Stephen. *Crescent and Star: Turkey between Two Worlds*. Rev. ed. New York: Farrar, Straus and Giroux, 2008.

Mansel, Philip. *Constantinople: City of the World's Desire, 1453–1924*. New York: St. Martin's Press, 1996.

Miszczak, Izabela. *Byzantine Secrets of Istanbul*. Istanbul: Viator Publications, 2020.

Miszczak, Izabela. *The Secrets of Ephesus*. Istanbul: Viator Publications, 2020.

Peirce, Leslie. *Empress of the East: How a European Slave Girl Became Queen of the Ottoman Empire*. New York: Basic Books, 2017.

Peirce, Leslie. *The Imperial Harem: Women and Sovereignty in the Ottoman Empire*. New York: Oxford University Press, 1993.

Pope, Nicole, and Hugh Pope. *Turkey Unveiled: A History of Modern Turkey*. Rev. ed. New York: Overlook Duckworth, 2011.

Potter, David. *Theodora: Actress, Empress, Saint*. New York: Oxford University Press, 2015.

ACKNOWLEDGEMENTS

What a privilege to have discovered a new way of inhabiting the world alongside my daughter, Sophie. Finding Theodora's monogram and then creating and leading the first *Lost Women of Turkey* trip together is something I'll always treasure.

The trip became a pilgrimage with the addition of my good friend and colleague, Tracy Johnson. Dreaming, building, leading, tattooing, researching, and adventuring together are among the greatest gifts I have known. The entire experience is richer for her presence.

And of course, a pilgrimage needs pilgrims. Thank you to the women who have said yes to traveling with us, entering uncomfortable, holy, and remarkable places with hunger and humility.

All of this—the research and curation of the feminine story— was encouraged and spurred on by my most faithful listeners, my family. Thank you, Chris, Aidan, Ella, and Sophie, for being such attentive students of my history lessons! And Ella, copyeditor extraordinaire, your eye for detail is a blessing!

For the processing, metabolizing, and metaphoring, for the cost and memory and story only we will ever share, and for the continual work of finding self, I am always and forever grateful to my husband, Chris.

Lastly, as a lost woman myself, I am profoundly relieved to have discovered a womb-like, mother-hearted, female-affirming

God. Thank you for showing me yourself in caves and baths and behind bars, for rewriting narratives lost to a male-centered history, and for reawakening a truth I'll gladly share.

BETH BRUNO is a curator of the historical feminine story. You can find her doing that in her book, *A VOICE BECOMING: A Yearlong Mother-Daughter Journey into Passionate, Purposed Living* (Faith Words, 2018) and through boutique *Lost Women of Turkey/ Egypt Pilgrimage(s)*. She and her husband spent ten years on staff with a parachurch ministry, mainly in Turkey, which led to a deep commitment to the global voice. Returning from overseas, Beth earned her MA in international community development. She holds a BA from Northwestern University, where she and her husband met over a quarter century ago. They now live in Colorado, travel often to visit their three young adult children, and co-lead a counseling center focused on *restorying* narratives that help people come alive.

To find out how you can join a *Lost Women
Pilgrimage* visit www.bethbruno.org.